# The Truth They Won't Tell You (And Don't Want You To Know) About The EU

**Books by Vernon Coleman include:**

The Medicine Men (1975)
Paper Doctors (1976)
Stress Control (1978)
The Home Pharmacy (1980)
Aspirin or Ambulance (1980)
Face Values (1981)
The Good Medicine Guide (1982)
Bodypower (1983)
Thomas Winsden's Cricketing Almanack (1983)
Diary of a Cricket Lover (1984)
Bodysense (1984)
Life Without Tranquillisers (1985)
The Story Of Medicine (1985, 1998)
Mindpower (1986)
Addicts and Addictions (1986)
Dr Vernon Coleman's Guide To Alternative Medicine (1988)
Stress Management Techniques (1988)
Know Yourself (1988)
The Health Scandal (1988)
The 20 Minute Health Check (1989)
Sex For Everyone (1989)
Mind Over Body (1989)
Eat Green Lose Weight (1990)
How To Overcome Toxic Stress (1990)
Why Animal Experiments Must Stop (1991)
The Drugs Myth (1992)
Complete Guide To Sex (1993)
How to Conquer Backache (1993)
How to Conquer Pain (1993)
Betrayal of Trust (1994)
Know Your Drugs (1994, 1997)
Food for Thought (1994, revised edition 2000)
The Traditional Home Doctor (1994)
People Watching (1995)
Relief from IBS (1995)
The Parent's Handbook (1995)
Men in Dresses (1996)
Power over Cancer (1996)
Crossdressing (1996)
How to Conquer Arthritis (1996)
High Blood Pressure (1996)
How To Stop Your Doctor Killing You (1996, revised edition 2003)
Fighting For Animals (1996)

Alice and Other Friends (1996)
Spiritpower (1997)
How To Publish Your Own Book (1999)
How To Relax and Overcome Stress (1999)
Animal Rights – Human Wrongs (1999)
Superbody (1999)
Complete Guide to Life (2000)
Strange But True (2000)
Daily Inspirations (2000)
Stomach Problems: Relief At Last (2001)
How To Overcome Guilt (2001)
How To Live Longer (2001)
Sex (2001)
We Love Cats (2002)
England Our England (2002)
Rogue Nation (2003)
People Push Bottles Up Peaceniks (2003)
The Cats' Own Annual (2003)
Confronting The Global Bully (2004)
Saving England (2004)
Why Everything Is Going To Get Worse Before It Gets Better (2004)
The Secret Lives of Cats (2004)
The Cat Basket (2005)
The Truth They Won't Tell You (And Don't Want You To Know)
    About The EU (2005)

**novels**
The Village Cricket Tour (1990)
The Bilbury Chronicles (1992)
Bilbury Grange (1993)
Mrs Caldicot's Cabbage War (1993)
Bilbury Revels (1994)
Deadline (1994)
The Man Who Inherited a Golf Course (1995)
Bilbury Pie (1995)
Bilbury Country (1996)
Second Innings (1999)
Around the Wicket (2000)
It's Never Too Late (2001)
Paris In My Springtime (2002)
Mrs Caldicot's Knickerbocker Glory (2003)
Too Many Clubs And Not Enough Balls (2005)
Tunnel (1980, 2005)

**as Edward Vernon**
Practice Makes Perfect (1977)
Practise What You Preach (1978)
Getting Into Practice (1979)
Aphrodisiacs – An Owner's Manual (1983)

**with Alice**
Alice's Diary (1989)
Alice's Adventures (1992)

**with Donna Antoinette Coleman**
How To Conquer Health Problems Between Ages 50 and 120 (2003)
Health Secrets Doctors Share With Their Families (2005)

# The Truth They Won't Tell You (And Don't Want You To Know) About The EU

## Vernon Coleman

BLUE
BOOKS

Published by Blue Books, Publishing House, Trinity Place, Barnstaple, Devon EX32 9HG, England.

Reprinted 2006 (four times)

ISBN: 1 899726 50 0

A catalogue record for this book is available from the British Library.

Printed by 4word Ltd, Bristol

# Dedication

To Donna Antoinette, with all my love.

# Foreword

For decades I have campaigned about health care and food and on behalf of people and animals. During recent years I have noticed (I could hardly not) the introduction of many new laws. Most of these seemed to remove the rights of individuals and to increase the rights of bureaucrats, politicians and international corporations. As a campaigning writer I found life becoming increasingly difficult. Many of my books were very effectively banned – for no other reason than they told the truth.

It didn't take long to discover that most of the new legislation eroding our freedom, destroying our culture and damaging our ability to speak out came not from Westminster but from our Masters in Brussels. It became clear that the European Union (EU) was the reason for most of the bad things that were happening. England, I realised, would be a better, happier, healthier, richer place if the EU had never been invented, the nation had never joined and the voters had never been tricked into keeping the country in. It is no exaggeration to say that almost everything that has changed our society for the worse in recent decades is a consequence of our membership of the EU.

It became clear that attempting to campaign on behalf of people and animals was unlikely to be of much use while the

EU continued to exist, and continued to churn out thousands of new laws. I was reminded of the old tale of the man who spends his life fishing people out of the river and then, at the end of his life, realises that he would have been rather more effective if he'd walked up the bank and had a firm word with the chap who was throwing all the people in.

At this point I should, I think, make my personal position clear.

I am not so much 'for' anything as I am against totalitarianism and fascism. I don't want to convert the world to my way of thinking and I certainly don't want to rule the world. I don't even want to tell everyone else what to do.

What I do object to is being hemmed in by rules and regulations which have nothing to do with protecting society as a whole but everything to do with protecting the interests (mainly financial) of a few people who, it seems to me, have helped themselves to enough of our money and are quite rich enough and powerful enough already.

And I object to the hypocrisies of enforced multiculturalism and political correctness. Shakespeare, Mozart and Leonardo da Vinci are probably the three greatest European artists. But all three failed to make it onto the EU's euro notes. Mozart was rejected because he was a womaniser (considered politically incorrect). Shakespeare was turned down because he wrote the *Merchant of Venice* (which is considered to be rude to Jews). And da Vinci was rejected because he is said to have had a liking for young boys (if the boys had been older his place on the euro note would doubtless have been assured). And so instead of illustrating the euro notes with any or all of these cultural icons, the EU bureaucrats preferred to use some exceedingly dull and anonymous bits of bridge.

Freedom isn't something we are given by politicians. It is one of our few basic rights. It is something we must value and protect when it is threatened. You and I have rights as individuals which are being eroded (without our permission) by the people who run the EU. I believe that our freedom is now under greater threat than it was at any time during the 20th century. The EU is quite clearly a fascist organisation and I firmly believe that it is as much of a threat to our liberty and our way of life as were the Nazis of Hitler's national socialism party. Our fight against the European Union is a fight against totalitarianism, tyranny and fascism.

I value the history and culture of my country.

I don't think it is better than the history or culture of any other country, but it is different and it is worth protecting – I would, as a matter of record, also fight to defend the history and culture of other sovereign nations within the EU. That, after all, is what so many Englishmen and women fought for in the two world wars of the 20th century.

I would, I confess, much rather be writing about things other than the EU. But I have always been fired and motivated by the importance of personal freedom and by injustice and have written much, over the years, about animal and human rights. There is, I believe, little point in campaigning about other issues without also attacking the existence of the EU. The EU reaches into all aspects of our personal and professional lives. The true story of the EU is one of corruption, fraud and deceit.

Millions of people ignore what is happening. They do and say nothing for a variety of reasons. Some don't think the EU really affects them. Others don't have the energy to fight, and to stand up for their freedom. They are beaten down by daily drudgery – much of it produced, perhaps with that intention, by the EU. Most do and say nothing because they don't understand what is going on. They don't realise that every time they turn on the television or open a newspaper they are being lied to.

I've written this book solely because I want to expose the lies told by those who support the EU, and to give the truth a bit of an airing.

All books and articles take sides, though many writers pretend to be fair and balanced when they are not. Journalists are skilled at writing articles which appear to say one thing but which actually say the other. They are also adept at writing articles which appear to be fair and balanced but which are, in fact, designed to propose the very specific political interests and concerns of their corporate paymasters.

The advantage of writing something which is not going to be published by a corporation with 'interests' and 'agendas' is that I can tell the truth and express my views.

When I started to research this book I began collecting evidence of deceit, misinformation, corruption and dishonesty by governments, large companies and the EU.

I was concerned, in particular, with deceits which affect our freedom and our health.

After twelve months of research I had (almost literally) a room full of research notes. It is usually impossible to see the surface of my desk but it had become impossible to see the carpet. Cuttings, Internet printouts, letters, documents, journals, books and video-tapes were piled in perilously high stacks. There is so much corruption and deceit practised by and within the EU that it is impossible for one man to keep track of it all. The EU has made freedom a dirty word and has turned patriotism into a sin.

Within this book you will find many things I suspect the Government, the BBC and the national press won't tell you (and don't want you to know).

But these are things we should all know.

Tell your friends.

The EU is down and wounded. But it is by no means dead. After the French voted 'No' to the proposed new EU constitution there was a widespread assumption that the EU was finished. It isn't. It's just as alive and dangerous as ever. Many of the proposals put forward in the rejected constitution are being implemented anyway.

In every way, every day, the EU will betray you, steal from you, lie to you and take away your freedom. (This is true of our Government too, for most politicians seem incapable of differentiating between right and wrong.) You need have no loyalty to, or respect for, an organisation which treats you with such little honour and decency and whose employees (and beneficiaries) have such a diminished sense of public, civic or personal responsibility.

Let's finish off the EU before it gets up again, and rescue England from its evil clutches.

*Vernon Coleman, July 2005*

# 1

*'Despite the political, economic and cultural legacy that has perpetuated its name, England no longer officially exists as a country and enjoys no separate political status within the United Kingdom.'*
ENCYCLOPAEDIA BRITANNICA

# 2

Millions of people who were once proud to call themselves English, and who served their country selflessly and with pride, are discovering that in the new, distasteful EU world in which we live, we should not expect too much from our country.

A growing number of people who have always obeyed the law, always paid their taxes and always been prepared to lay down their lives for their country are discovering that, as they get older, they are made to feel like a drag on the community they have served so well.

Today it is, I fear, foolish to think for a moment that your nation really cares about you (except as a source of labour and money). It does not.

The England we respected and loved is in hibernation.

Our nation (now recreated by the EU and represented by the politicians and civil servants who control the finances and the administration) does not care one jot about history or culture. Nor does it care about the elderly and the genuinely needy.

The State's priority – and indeed 'right' as understood by the politicians and the civil servants – is to take and not to give.

You have to get used to the fact that your nation will ruthlessly use you, eviscerate you and suck you dry. You must never expect an ounce of compassion from the State or its servants, for nations are personified not by the magnanimous and honourable (generous deeds are always performed by individuals and never by nations) but by the little men: the rule makers, the clerks and the self-serving hypocrites who claim to be concerned with the greater good but who are in practice concerned only with satisfying their own never-diminishing greed.

The practical significance of all this is that the only people who are reliably interested in your health and survival are you and those who care about you. You must learn to take responsibility for your own health and welfare: to look after your mind, body and soul yourself. The only other individuals whom you can truly trust are the people who love you and care for you. A significant consequence of this is that your primary loyalty should be not be to a state or nation but to the people who are genuinely and lovingly close to you.

That's the present. That's the world we live in now.

But if we fight hard we can and will take back our nation from the EU.

We can reclaim the England we love and respect.

We can put dignity and pride back into our feelings for our nation.

## 3

When England won the rugby world cup an EU spokesperson described the success as a great victory for Europe. Pro-EU politicians found the victory extremely embarrassing because it led to a temporary increase in flag waving nationalist fervour.

## 4

*'England is divided into eight geographic regions, often referred to as the standard regions of England...'*
ENCYCLOPAEDIA BRITANNICA

## 5

The EU is determined to 'kill off' England (and the English). The English are the constant victims of rampant racism. They are, indeed, now perhaps Europe's most persecuted minority.

Does that not make the EU, and those who support it, guilty of racism and genocide?

## 6

The monstrous war criminal Blair stopped other party leaders and the monarch, Queen Elizabeth II, from attending the Victory in Europe memorial commemoration at the Cenotaph on 8th May 2005.

The event had been organised months earlier to mark the 60th anniversary of Victory in Europe Day.

Blair (a man who lives for photo opportunities more than any other politician in history) pulled out of the event and the other party leaders were then duly disinvited. Our Prime Minister chose instead to spend the weekend at 'his' country house.

One courtier is quoted as having said that the Queen was 'hurt and puzzled' at being stopped from attending the VE Day celebrations.

She may well be hurt but she shouldn't be puzzled.

The Queen has, after all, received (and effectively ignored) sackfuls of letters complaining about the way that English history is being suppressed in the name of the EU.

# 7

England is being officially airbrushed out of existence.

The last census form, distributed to all British homes at the turn of the millennium, allowed citizens to describe their nationality, heritage and ethnic background as Scottish, Welsh, Irish, Chinese, Caribbean, Indian, Pakistani – virtually anything you can think of.

But not English.

There was no space on the form for anyone to describe themselves as 'English'.

Why?

Simple.

The EU does not want England to exist. The EU's plan is for England to become nine separate regions.

This overt example of racism or ethnic cleansing (the attempted destruction of an entire race is also described as genocide) continues on countless application forms (particularly ones where people are being invited to apply for official or quasi-official posts) where applicants are requested to indicate their ethnic background. You can tick Scottish, Irish, Welsh, White and Black Caribbean, White or Black African, White or Asian Indian, Pakistani, Other European or British. But you will hardly ever find a box enabling you to describe yourself as English.

Do you really think it is a coincidence that at the same time as all this goes on, English history has been airbrushed out of our educational system? Do you think it is merely unfortunate that 'new' English citizens are required to have a working knowledge of benefits legislation but not to have even a rudimentary knowledge of English history? Do you really think it is merely 'silly' that it is legal to fly any flag you like – except the English flag?

We are witnessing a silent holocaust of English culture; an EU inspired bout of racial cleansing.

## 8

When students at one English University wanted to start an English society they were told that they couldn't.

To support or celebrate anything English is likely to result in a ban.

## 9

*'We call our islands by no less than six different names, England, Britain, Great Britain, the British Isles, the United Kingdom and, in very exalted moments, Albion.'*
GEORGE ORWELL (*THE LION AND THE UNICORN*)

## 10

Both the Scottish and Welsh nationalists blame all the bad stuff in their history on England and the English. All these extremists seem to believe that only the EU can offer them the independence they crave. (The vast majority of Scottish and Welsh citizens regard the Welsh and Scottish nationalists as irrelevant and rather potty. But, in Wales and Scotland as elsewhere, it is the potent and malevolent few who run things these days.) They are all deluded, of course. Membership of the EU means that the Welsh and the Scots have no chance of achieving real independence. Their dream of having their own real parliament is now further away than ever. But they don't realise this and they won't accept it as the truth. They have been misled by promises and bribed by gold from Brussels. (The supply of gold is now finished since the EU needs to distribute its takings to the East Europeans and the Welsh and the Scots will receive nothing in the future. But the promises and the temptations will continue.)

So, the bottom line is that there isn't much of a future for Britain or for the United Kingdom which has, let's face it, always been as loose and as uncomfortable an amalgam of nations as the USSR or, indeed, the EU. The UK was created only because of the physical proximity of the members and the fact of their sharing an island. Only the English now describe themselves as British.

The United Kingdom Independence Party may dream of glories (and independence) for the United Kingdom but although our past may have been as Britain our only future is as England.

# 11

In an attempt to bring Regional Assemblies out into the open, and to make them acceptable to English voters, the Labour Government decided to have a referendum in the North East; to ask the people there if they wanted to have a Regional Assembly. Labour chose the North East because they thought that was where they stood the best chance of winning the vote. They spent a lot of time and public money campaigning for a 'yes' vote. The Government never mentioned that the Regional Assembly was part of the EU plan for a United States of Europe. Nor, as far as I am aware, did any national newspaper, national TV or radio station.

When the people of the North East voted on whether or not they wanted a Regional Assembly, 197,310 voted 'for' and 696,519 voted 'against'. It was a humiliating defeat for the EU, for Labour and for Prescott (who had 'masterminded' and spearheaded the 'yes' campaign).

But, despite the resounding 'no' vote, the North East of England has a Regional Assembly.

The Regional Assembly building was already fully staffed and operational when the people of the North East were asked to decide whether or not they wanted one.

That's democracy EU and Labour style.

How appropriate that Prescott's humiliating defeat at the hands of voters in the North East should have taken place on November 5th 2004 – the night when the English celebrate

Guy Fawkes's attempt to destroy Parliament.

The fascist Labour Government naturally pretended that the unsuccessful attempt to force a Regional Assembly on the people of the North East was an act of political generosity on their part. Their line was that the voters of the North East had stupidly turned down a great gift.

Politicians and national media all carefully avoided the truth; which is that the North Eastern Regional mini-parliament already exists. As do other Regional mini-parliaments around the country. They may be secret. The members may be unelected. But they already exist.

And both politicians and the national media also carefully avoided the fact that these new Regional Assemblies are nothing to do with providing an extra layer of political representation for English voters but are simply part of the EU's plan to get rid of England and the House of Commons and to replace the former with nine EU regions and the latter with nine regional EU parliaments.

The significance of the rout of Prescott cannot be over-estimated. This was one of the most important votes in England's history. (You wouldn't know this from the way the English media dealt with the election. Not one TV network ran a programme dealing with the election. I didn't see one national newspaper with the vote result on its front page the next day.)

Europhiles were said to be devastated.

But they did not, of course, close down the Regional Assemblies they had already set up and which already had buildings, staff, members, huge budgets and power.

Including the one in the North East of England.

## 12

*'England is perhaps the only great country whose intellectuals are
ashamed of their own nationality. In left-wing circles it is always felt
that there is something slightly disgraceful in being an Englishman and
that it is a duty to snigger at every English institution, from
horse racing to suet puddings. It is a strange fact, but it is
unquestionably true that almost any English intellectual would
feel more ashamed of standing to attention during 'God Save
the King' than of stealing from a poor box.'*
GEORGE ORWELL (*THE LION AND THE UNICORN*)

## 13

England has no parliament and some campaigners believe it
should have. What those campaigners don't usually realise,
however, is that there is no English Parliament because if the
EU gets its way there will be no England. There will, instead,
be a series of featureless, characterless regions – each with its
own regional assembly. How can I prove this? Easy. The nine
regional assemblies already exist. One of them, the London
Assembly is functioning. The other eight exist in secret –
though they are being given increasing amounts of power by
the Labour Government.

## 14

Our Parliament at Westminster is subordinate to the European
Commission in Brussels from whence comes a constant torrent
of new regulations.

They are called 'regulations' but, make no mistake about
it, they are 'laws'. Regulations from the EU come with the
strength of law. They are undeniable and unalterable. They
have to be passed by our own Parliament at Westminster which
now sits as a huge rubber-stamping machine.

Politicians at Westminster take responsibility for the new

laws from the EU (even though they may not agree with them) because they know that they have no choice. And if they are seen to question the laws which emanate from Brussels they will expose the whole sham that is now the English Parliament. English civil servants now exist not to oversee new laws passed by English politicians but to oversee new laws passed by EU civil servants.

The constant flow of new laws is designed to help increase the speed of integration, to cement the power of the European Commission and to keep us occupied with minutiae so that we do not have time to realise what is happening. We are kept so busy worrying about the size of our duck eggs and the shape of our bananas that we have no time left to reflect on the loss of our freedom, our independence and our sovereignty. Ignorance of the law is no excuse for breaking the law. How can anyone possibly know all of the 100,000 laws which we have been given by the EU? How can anyone possibly be familiar with the endless rulings, technicalities and amendments? We've come a long way from the ten commandments.

## 15

*'Like all other modern people, the English are in process of being numbered, labelled, conscripted, 'coordinated'. But the pull of their impulses is in the other direction, and the kind of regimentation that can be imposed on them will be modified in consequence.'*
GEORGE ORWELL (*THE LION AND THE UNICORN*)

## 16

It is now clear that our traditional currency (pounds, shillings and pence) were got rid of in order to prepare us for entry into the euro.

## 17

*'For the People...truly I desire their liberty and freedom as much as anybody whosoever; but I must tell you, that their liberty and freedom consist in having of Government, those laws, by which their life and their goods may be most their own. It is not for having share in Government that is nothing pertaining to them.'*
CHARLES I, SPEAKING ON THE SCAFFOLD BEFORE HIS
EXECUTION IN 1649

## 18

Famous old English army regiments are disappearing because they have to make way for the European Army or Rapid Reaction Force (formed as a result of the Amsterdam Treaty in 1999). The distribution of the EU's regional defence forces will fit in nicely with the unelected Regional Assemblies which we already have.

## 19

Now that (courtesy of the EU) Scotland, Wales and Northern Ireland all have their own assemblies (they are allowed to call them parliaments) many nationalists in those countries believe that they have won a sort of independence and that their parliaments are the first step towards self-rule. Oh dear. They are so wrong. Their assemblies/parliaments exist only because the EU wants them to exist. In the United States of Europe, Scotland, Wales and Northern Ireland will all be regions with their own regional parliaments.

Welsh and Scottish nationalists should fight hard to save England.

Millions of Welsh and Scottish nationalists believe that now that they have their own parliaments they are well on the way to independence.

Nothing could be further from the truth.

The Welsh and the Scottish have never had it so good.

And soon they will realise just how much they should have loved England.

In Scotland, students get free university education (paid for by English taxpayers). In England, students have to pay their own university fees. In Scotland, the elderly get free nursing home care (paid for by English taxpayers). In England, the elderly have to pay their own nursing home fees. In Wales, prescription costs are heavily subsidised and there is talk in the Welsh Parliament of doing away with the prescription charge completely. Who pays for all this? English taxpayers help a great deal. In England, taxpayers have to pay much more for a prescription. English taxpayers have for years subsidised Wales and Scotland. Every man, woman and child in Scotland is effectively given £30 a week by English taxpayers. The chances are that without the help of English taxpayers the Welsh nationalists would not be able to insist that all official documents and road signs be produced in Welsh as well as English.

Welsh and Scottish Nationalists (who, because of their activity and belligerence have a political and financial influence in their countries far greater than their constituency should allow them) believe that even if their newfound semi-independence is limited to being regions within the ever enlarging EU they will be better off in the future than they were when they were joined with England as part of the United Kingdom.

Wrong.

Badly wrong.

As more and more poorer countries (Poland, Romania, Turkey etc.) join the EU so the amount of money available to Wales and Scotland will diminish. I suspect that before long both Wales and Scotland will be net *contributors* to the EU. The Welsh and Scottish will end up sending money to Turkey – in just the same way as, in the past, the English have sent money to Wales and Scotland. They will then long for the days when they received (as they do now) massive subsidies from English taxpayers.

Wales and Scotland will grow to rue the day when the UK was broken up. They will eventually realise that giving them their 'independence' was merely a trick to break up the UK into tiny EU regions.

If Welsh and Scottish nationalists have any sense at all they will fight now to destroy the EU and to keep England alive and healthy.

None of the nine regions which will replace England will be able (or willing) to carry on making massive charitable contributions to Wales and Scotland.

Scottish and Welsh nationalists don't give a damn about Great Britain or the United Kingdom. And they certainly don't care about England – or what happens to her. They don't understand that their future is now very much dependent upon what happens to the United Kingdom in general – and to England in particular. The Scottish and Welsh nationalists care only for their own individual nations.

But the bottom line is that without England, Wales and Scotland are stuffed. And the EU is not their friend. The EU recently published a map of EU countries. They forgot to include Wales.

## 20

Having a fascist and totalitarian English Government is bad enough. Having a fascist and totalitarian European Government would be even worse.

## 21

*'We see the EU not as clog-footed woodenheads but as a help and protection against both 'little England' and 'big America'.'*
LETTER FROM SCOTSMAN ATTACKING ME FOR WRITING AND PUBLISHING *ENGLAND OUR ENGLAND*.

# 22

For years now men and women from Scotland have dominated English politics and public life. Since the Scots now have their own parliament this domination is impossible to justify.

Blair, of course, is Scottish (though he does his best to conceal his roots). He was born and went to public school in Scotland. (He went to Fettes, often called the Scottish Eton.) He is the leader of the McMafia. Ministers in charge of Transport and Health have been Scottish even though neither ministry has any responsibility in Scotland. A Scottish Health Secretary, supported by votes from Scottish backbenchers, imposed hospital trusts on England while Scotland remained exempt. It was Scottish MPs who helped ensure that students in England have to pay tuition fees while students in Scotland are exempt. The Liberals are led by a Scot. The speaker of Parliament, Michael Martin, is a Scot. Leading Scottish politicians include Gordon Brown and the late Robin Cook. Scots from Scottish constituencies have power in Westminster and vote on issues which affect England alone. Many English constituencies are held by Scots. (Though woe betide Englishmen or women who try to stand for election to represent Scottish seats.) Three Scots in succession (Lords Mackay, Irvine and Falconer) led the English legal system (the Scots have their own). There have been four Scottish Archbishops of Canterbury leading the Church of England though there would, of course, never be (and certainly never has been) an English Moderator of the Church of Scotland. The Scottish Parliament is very much a parliament of Scots. There are 400,000 English people living in Scotland but only a handful of English people sit in their parliament. Many English quangos, think tanks and pressure groups are run by Scots. Many were given their power by Blair. Large sections of the media are controlled by Scots. Many of the Scots who have abandoned their home country and come to England seeking, and acquiring, fame fortune and power are assertive, arrogant and violently anti-English. At the 2005 general election (to elect a Prime Minister for England, since Scotland, Wales and Northern Ireland have their own parliaments) the candidates for the three main parties were two Scotsmen and a Welshman of Transylvanian origins. This is not a question of foreign politicians being less competent than English ones. The point is simply that they may be likely be less passionate about England than an English politician would.

This is all so unprecedented that it is reasonable to ask if there could be a purpose in what is happening.

Well, maybe there could.

Oppressing, suppressing and ultimately obliterating England and the English is an important part of the EU's plan. For the EU project to be safely completed England must disappear.

# 23

If the planned EU constitution (which Blair *et al* have already signed) is ever brought into action it will be impossible for Scotland ever to become an independent state. The Spanish plan to use the constitution's provisions on 'territorial integrity' to make sure that Basque nationalists cannot have an independent Basque state recognised by the EU.

The Scots, who hate the English and think that the EU offers their country an independent future, are missing the point because, however much they may hate the English and for whatever reasons (real or imagined) the big, urgent and very real threat to their country comes from the EU.

## 24

*'But talk to foreigners, read foreign books or newspapers, and you are brought back to the same thought. Yes, there is something distinctive and recognisable in English civilisation. It is a culture as individual as that of Spain. It is somehow bound up with solid breakfasts and gloomy Sundays, smoky towns and winding roads, green fields and red pillar boxes. It has a flavour of its own. Moreover it is continuous, it stretches into the future and the past, there is something in it that persists, as in a living creature. What can the England of 1940 have in common with the England of 1840? But then, what have you in common with the child of five whose photograph your mother keeps on the mantelpiece? Nothing, except that you happen to be the same person. And above all it is your civilisation, it is you. However much you hate it or laugh at it, you will never be happy away from it for any length of time. The suet puddings and the red pillar boxes have entered into your soul. Good or evil, it is yours, you belong to it, and this side the grave you will never get away from the marks that it has given you.'*
GEORGE ORWELL, (*THE LION AND THE UNICORN*)

## 25

The word 'fascism' is often used as a term of abuse for anyone who opposes the EU. For example, those who care about England are sometimes described as fascists by supporters of the EU. This is, of course, self-serving nonsense. If nationalism is fascism then Scottish and Welsh nationalists must be fascists too. The evidence shows quite clearly that the EU is a truly fascist organisation and the people who work for it and support it are, therefore, the fascists.

## 26

It is perhaps not widely known but the English press helped trick the electorate into supporting England's entry into the

Common Market. And once we had been taken in, it was the press which encouraged Britons to vote 'Yes' to stay in the Common Market.

By 1971, it was obvious that most English newspapers were wildly committed to England becoming a member of the EEC. Only the *Express* titles were not clamouring for membership.

The *Financial Times* and the *Daily Mirror* had both been strong advocates of membership from the early 1960s before leading politicians took to the idea.

The first Prime Minister to try to lead England into the EEC was Harold Wilson who, from 1966, was convinced that England could not survive outside the EEC. His Government's application to join, in May 1967, was vetoed by General de Gaulle, the French president, whose life and career had been saved by the English during the Second World War. Actually, French President Charles de Gaulle rejected England's application to join the Common Market twice. In public he argued that England, a traditional island nation, was not suited to be part of a European superstate. That was just political flim-flam. In reality he rejected England (despite everything that England had done for him and France during the Second World War) because he wanted to delay England's entry until the Common Agricultural Policy (designed to give huge subsidies to French peasant farmers) had been properly set up. Once the CAP was in place the loathsome de Gaulle suddenly decided that England's island history no longer mattered and he became enthusiastic about England joining the Common Market. Naturally, he really wanted England to join the Market in order to help pay for the costs of running the CAP and keeping French farmers satisfied. Right from the start of the EU England has been used by both America and France. And it is still happening.

Three years later, when the foul and repulsive Ted Heath

got into Number 10 Downing Street he began negotiations again and a treaty was agreed in January 1972. This was the infamous treaty in which the treasonous Heath lied to everyone and betrayed his country.

In the months prior to Heath's betrayal, the English public had not been convinced that they wanted their country to enter the EEC. Many, perhaps, simply didn't trust the politicians' claims that membership would be merely a commercial convenience. One opinion poll in early 1971 showed that the English people were against entry by the astonishing ratio of three to one. This opposition came despite the expenditure by the European Commission Information Service of around £10 million on trying to persuade opinion formers of the benefits of membership of the EEC.

With it looking as though joining the EEC might be political suicide the Government became desperate. Heath's Government paid for the distribution of propaganda extolling the virtues of membership and produced a White Paper which was full of unsubstantiated claims for the EEC and which deliberately omitted any mention of the costs of membership or the fact that joining the EEC was the first step towards a federal states of Europe.

Heath only got away with his Great Betrayal because the press had decided that entry was a 'good thing' (for them and their proprietors) and so did not question any of the claims made by Heath's Government.

Editors and columnists slavishly obeyed the dictates of their proprietors. If the press had done its job properly England would have almost certainly never joined the EEC and would now be a considerably wealthier and more powerful nation.

The *Financial Times*, the *Times*, the *Guardian*, the *Daily Telegraph*, the *Sunday Times*, the *Observer*, the *Daily Mail*, the *Sun* and *The Economist* were all wildly enthusiastic about England joining the EEC. (As, indeed, most of them still are.) Throughout the run up to the day of our joining, the daily news in England was delivered with a preposterous pro-EEC slant designed to suppress the truth and to convince the public that without membership of the EEC neither they nor their country had much of a future. Only occasionally did the papers admit that the politicians were spinning like tops. The *Times* remarked that Geoffrey Rippon, the Cabinet Minister responsible for negotiating England's entry, was behaving 'almost as though he has something to hide'. (He certainly did.) The *Daily Mirror* (which, at the time, had by far the largest sale in England) was unrelenting in describing the prizes of membership as immense and warning readers that if they voted against membership of the EEC they would become 'mere lookers-on from an off-shore island of dwindling insignificance'.'

When Prince Philip claimed that the EEC's Common Agricultural Policy was an example of bad management the *Daily Mirror* called him a 'chump'. (So, now who's the chump?)

The pro-EEC line appeared on news and feature pages and was supplemented with huge numbers of full page advertisements paid for by the European Movement.

Heath took England into the EEC with the help of the nation's press and without ever giving the electors a chance to say whether or not their country should become part of the European 'project'.

Only the *Daily Express* 'stood alone – with the people' against membership of the EEC. They praised Philip's scepticism about the Common Agricultural Policy announcing that 'The people applaud his good sense...and wish it were more widely shared by our rulers.' But once the vote for membership had been won even the *Daily Express* capitulated and accepted the verdict.

When, at the next election Heath was thrown out by the English electorate the subsequent Prime Minister, crafty, pipe-sucking Harold Wilson, agreed to the unprecedented idea of asking the English people for their view on membership; he announced that there would be a referendum to decide whether or not England should remain in the EEC. (The referendum appeared in the Labour Party's 1974 election manifesto and may well have one of the reasons for Wilson's victory.)

This was the first and last chance the English people had to express their view on the EEC. (For the record I am delighted to report that I voted 'No' – against the EEC. It seemed to me pretty obvious that the politicians were lying and planning something considerably more sinister than a trading partnership.)

The question to be asked in the referendum was simple: 'Do you think that the United Kingdom should stay in the European Community (the Common Market)?'

The referendum vote took place in June 1975 and virtually the whole of the English press joined in to extol the virtues of membership of the EEC. Even the *Daily Express* now joined the other papers in support of the EEC. Of England's national press only the *Morning Star* campaigned against the EEC.

During the run up to the referendum the press either supported the 'Yes' vote campaigners or ignored the campaign completely. When Tony Benn accurately revealed that almost half a million jobs had been lost in England since the country had entered the Common Market, and correctly predicted that many jobs would be lost if we stayed in, the papers dismissed his claim as nonsense. The *Daily Mirror*, for example, sneered about 'lies, more lies and those damned statistics'. The *Daily Telegraph* nauseatingly talked about 'an intellectual, moral and spiritual value' in the EEC. The *Financial Times* predictably quoted John Donne ('no man is an island') and argued that to leave the EEC 'would be a gratuitous act of irresponsible folly'. The *Guardian* described the referendum as 'a vote for the next century'. The *Daily Mail* told its readers to 'Vote YES for Britain'. The *Daily Express* announced: 'The *Express* is for the market'. The *Sun* told readers: 'Yes for a future together. No for a future alone.'

In the days before the crucial vote the national papers had, between them, 188 front pages. Disgracefully, only 33 of those front pages were devoted to the most important vote in England's history.

On the day of the vote the *Daily Mail* (which now likes to portray itself as a committed opponent of the EU) didn't even put the referendum on its front page. The *Daily Mirror's* front page on polling day screamed: 'A Vote for the Future'. Inside the *Mirror* had a picture of nine pupils at an international school in Brussels, one child from each EEC country. Eight of the children stood together, cuddling and cosy. The ninth child stood alone, isolated and sad. 'He's the odd lad out,' said The *Mirror*. 'The boy beyond the fringe. The one whose country still has to make up its mind. For the lad outside, vote yes.'

The vast majority of the material printed in the national press was supportive of the EEC and dismissive of those who questioned the value of membership. There was no debate and the result, therefore, was a foregone conclusion. The political establishment, big business and the press conspired to suppress the truth and to 'sell' the electorate a ragbag of lies.

This was, in my view, the beginning of the end for the independence and integrity of the English press. Newspaper proprietors have always used their papers to promote their own views, often for their own commercial advantage, but this was I believe the first time that the English press had united to support such a sinister and dishonest purpose. If journalists did not know that they were encouraging the English people to hand over their independence they were incompetent and stupid. If they knew but did it anyway then they were as guilty of treason as Heath, Rippon and the long tawdry line of English Prime Ministers and Ministers who have followed them.

The result was a foregone conclusion.

Conned, tricked, lied to and spun into a world which bore no resemblance to reality, the English people voted to stay in the Common Market. A total of 17.3 million voted 'yes' and 8.4 million voted 'no'. The establishment, aided and abetted by the press, had turned a massive suspicion and disapproval of the common market into a huge level of support.

It was the English press which helped lying, cheating, conniving politicians trick the electorate into accepting membership of the EEC.

How many people would have voted for the EEC if they had known the truth?

## 27

It has been revealed that prior to the signing of the Treaty of Rome, England's Lord Chancellor wrote to Prime Minister Edward Heath with this warning: 'I must emphasise that in my view the surrenders of sovereignty involved are serious ones...these objections ought to be brought out into the open.'

Heath, who should have been hung as a traitor, assured the nation that there would be no loss of sovereignty.

## 28

One bizarre and revealing slogan from the 1975 pro-Common Market campaign was: 'Better to lose a little sovereignty than to lose a son or daughter.' The slogan showed that the proponents of the Common Market were admitting that there would be a loss of sovereignty if we stayed in the Common Market. The reference to losing 'a son or daughter' was intended to imply that if we didn't stay in the Common Market we might somehow find ourselves at war with Germany or France.

## 29

The EU has expanded a great deal in a relatively short period of time. It started life as a simple coal-and-steel community in the early 1950s. By the time England joined it had become a Common Market, designed to help encourage trade between selected European countries. When Britons got a chance to vote on whether or not the country should stay in the Common Market there were no *outward* signs that the EEC was about to metamorphose into a United States of Europe.

Today, bit by bit, the EU has acquired a currency, a central bank, a parliament, a civil service, a supreme court, a military staff and an army, its own police force, a flag, a diplomatic corps and an anthem. (I wonder how many people know that the EU already has its own anthem. Why would the EU need an anthem if it wasn't planning to become a 'country'?)

The changes have taken place with hardly a whimper of protest. There have been very few electoral revolts against European integration. Most taxpayers know very little of the EU or the impact it is having on their lives. Most assume (erroneously) that the new laws they dislike come from their own governments. There are no mainstream political parties opposing or even questioning the aims and targets of the EU.

However, throughout Europe, people don't much like the idea of the EU. In Germany, one of the founder members, around 40% of voters think their country has benefited from EU membership but another 40% think it hasn't. In Spain, the referendum on the new EU constitution was won with the vast majority of voters admitting that they didn't have the faintest idea what the constitution included or, indeed, what the EU did or was for. The citizens of France are so unenthusiastic about the EU that huge numbers of shops still display prices in francs as well as euros, even though the French franc has been of only historical interest for several years. A poll taken throughout Europe showed that around half of the electorate would be 'very relieved' or wouldn't mind if the EU simply disappeared.

The Swedes and the Danes both voted against adopting the euro. Three quarters of Britons dislike the EU and in most other EU countries the EU has a positive image among less than half the electorate.

Where governments have offered their citizens a referendum on EU issues the results have been largely negative. The people of Ireland have probably benefited more from the EU than the citizens of most other countries and yet when the Irish Government gave voters a chance to express their views on the Nice Treaty (a flawed attempt to modernise the EU, which paved the way for a recent EU expansion) the voters roundly rejected the Treaty. The Irish Government and the EU had to do some fancy dancing and have a second vote in order to get the Irish people to come up with the 'right' answer. (Forcing a second vote when the first vote doesn't produce the right result is becoming increasingly common. When the Danes voted 'No' to the Masstricht Treaty in 1992 they were given a 'second chance' and duly voted 'Yes' in 1993. It was the Masstricht Treaty which paved the way for a common foreign policy and for the euro. In England even the Marylebone Cricket Club resorted to multiple voting in order to get the answer it wanted when members initially said 'No' to admitting women members.)

The EU has been foisted on us without our understanding and against our will. We have been lied to, deceived and cheated by whole generations of European and English politicians. Every English Minister from Ted Heath onwards should be locked in the Tower of London and charged with treason.

The EU simply isn't what they said it was going to be.

We were sold a trading partnership.

We've been given a federal Europe.

## 30

*'Seven multinational companies or wealthy families own all the mass
circulation newspapers in Britain. Generally speaking, they use their
papers to campaign single-mindedly in defence of their commercial
interests and the political policies which will protect them.'*
TONY BENN, 1981

## 31

The European Commission helped to fund the 'Yes' campaign
in 1975 when Britons voted on whether or not to stay in the
Common Market. This is like allowing an accused man and
his friends to sit on the jury. When England was preparing for
a referendum on the EU constitution the European
Commission once again provided funds to help the 'Yes'
campaign.

What can be more corrupt than a public body using
taxpayers' funds to pay to influence a vote in its favour?

## 32

In 1776 Adam Waishaupt suggested that the 'elite' members
of the population should take over the world.

His plan for world domination contained seven basic points:

1. Abolition of all individual governments.
2. Abolition of private property.
3. Abolition of inheritance.
4. Abolition of patriotism.
5. Abolition of religion.
6. Abolition of the idea of the family,
7. Creation of a world government.

These plans have been adopted by many secret
organisations now active in geopolitical affairs.

The EU's policies and aims seem to fit well into Waishaupt's
plan.

# 33

Individual countries could not agree on what the planned new EU constitution did and did not say. The English Government said that the constitution's new Charter of Fundamental Rights did not limit the rights of managers to sack workers. But the French and the Belgians said the charter of Fundamental Rights did limit the rights of managers to sack workers. The English Government said that the Constitution would end all speculation about a common EU tax. 'The Constitution shows that there are no plans for a common EU tax,' said the English Government. This is not quite what the Belgian Government (and others) said. They said that the EU was heading for a common tax.

On February 25th 2005, Germany's Foreign Minister confirmed that the new EU constitution was intended to create a new European country. Hans Martin Bury said the treaty was the 'birth certificate' for a giant superstate, and a 'framework for an ever closer union'.

Two weeks earlier, English Foreign Minister Jack Straw had said that the treaty would bolster England's sovereign rights. The Labour Government claimed that the new EU constitution was merely a 'tidying up' exercise.

The new EU constitution has been described as the 'birth certificate of the United States of Europe' by Hans Martin Bury, whose words should be taken seriously for he spoke as Germany's Europe minister. In sharp contrast to New Labour's claim that the EU constitution was just a tidying up exercise, Herr Bury said that the constitution was 'more than just a milestone'. 'It is...', he said, 'the framework for – as it says in the preamble – an ever closer union.'

In 2003, German Foreign Minister Joschka Fischer said that the new EU constitution was 'the most important treaty since the formation of the European Economic Community'.

The EU constitution was not about changing xenophobic European nations into a multi-cultural superstate (though that was part of it). It was about getting rid of free markets, small governments and freedom and replacing them (because they are seen by the EU federalists as 'messy' and 'inefficient') with a centralised, protectionist state managed by bureaucrats.

When the new EU constitution was signed by national leaders, the original plan was for the EU nations (all 25 of them) to agree on a common declaration, explaining what the EU constitution would (and would not do).

Unfortunately, the 25 nations couldn't agree on what to put in the declaration. They couldn't agree on this because they couldn't agree on what the EU constitution contained or on what it would do.

So each country 'interpreted' the new EU constitution in its own way; in the way each Government thought would best suit the mood and hopes of its voters.

The significant lesson for us all from the EU Constitution is that politicians lied, without hesitation, when explaining to their citizens precisely what the Constitution contained and would do.

How can it ever be possible to trust anything a politician says about the EU?

## 34

*'We are with Europe, but not of it. We are linked, but not compromised. We are interested and associated but not absorbed...
For we dwell among our own people.'*
WINSTON CHURCHILL, RESPONDING TO THE IDEA
OF EUROPEAN UNITY IN 1948.

## 35

*'This constitution marks a shift from a primarily economic Europe to a political Europe.'*
JOSEP BORRELL, SPANISH PRESIDENT OF
THE EUROPEAN PARLIAMENT

## 36

*'The EU constitution represents 'a great step forward for the EU to become a true political union'.'*
JEAN-LUC DEHAENE, BELGIAN VICE-PRESIDENT OF THE CONVENTION WHICH DRAFTED THE EU CONSTITUTION

## 37

*'The EU constitution is 'an expression of Europe as a union of nation-states...the rejection of Europe as a federal superstate'.'*
TONY BLAIR, WAR CRIMINAL AND LIAR

## 38

*'Member States shall actively and unreservedly support the European Union's foreign and security policy.'*
FROM THE EU'S NEW (2005) CONSTITUTION

## 39

*'The last time Britain went into Europe with any degree of success was on 6th June 1944.'*
DAILY EXPRESS, 1980

## 40

Prior to the General Election in May 2005, the English Government allocated £495,000 of taxpayers' money for a PR drive to promote the EU constitution. Some of the money was allocated for signing up celebrities as 'champions of the EU Constitution'.

## 41

*'What good fortune for governments that the people do not think.'*
ADOLF HITLER

## 42

*'It (is) impossible for Britain to accept the principle, that the most economic forces of this country should be handed over to an authority that is utterly undemocratic and is responsible to nobody.'*
CLEMENT ATTLEE, LABOUR PRIME MINISTER
RESPONDING TO THE SCHUMAN PLAN FOR THE EUROPEAN
COAL AND STEEL COMMUNITY IN 1950.

## 43

The Labour slogan 'Forwards not Backwards' was stolen from the East German communists.

## 44

Among other things the proposed new EU constitution recommends:

♦ Europe-wide taxes (probably on top of national taxes).
♦ Massive increases in worker' rights – even guaranteeing a job for life.
♦ A Europe-wide minimum wage.
♦ A common education curriculum throughout the EU (which must include pro-EU propaganda).
♦ A more powerful EU army.
♦ The abolition of national sovereignty.
♦ A huge rise in the EU budget.
♦ Recognition that the new constitution is regarded as the first step towards political unity.

I feel sure that the Labour Government meant to tell you about these things. Perhaps they just forgot. Or were too busy waging war. Or thought that if they just kept declaring war (illegally) on small, harmless countries no one would notice what the EU constitution contained.

## 45

*'The Union shall have exclusive competence over...monetary policy, commercial policy, Customs Union.'*
FROM THE EU'S NEW (2005) CONSTITUTION

## 46

*'EU law shall have primacy over the law of member States.'*
FROM THE EU'S NEW (2005) CONSTITUTION

## 47

The wars against Iraq, Afghanistan and Kosovo were a perfect distraction from the real enemy: the proponents of the EU project.

England is the most anti-EU member nation. Our Government desperately needed to stop us worrying about Europe, and to encourage us to worry about other things.

## 48

In an attempt to persuade the French to vote 'Yes' for the EU constitution, the EU went for something it understands well – bribery and corruption. The French were offered a cut in VAT on restaurant bills from 19.6% to 5.5%.

It is to their lasting credit that the French were not so easily bribed.

## 49

Immediately after the French voted 'No' to the EU constitution it was EU Commissioner (and disgraced British politician) Peter Mandelson who was alleged to have been among the first to have the arrogance and the indifference to public opinion to suggest that the French Government hold a second referendum so that the French people would have a second chance to get the right answer. A couple of days later, when the Dutch added their disapproving voice, rejecting the EU constitution with a massive majority, Jean-Claude Juncker, the Luxembourg Prime Minister insisted that the constitution was still alive and that he wanted both France and Holland to vote again so that they could give 'the right answer'. He added that he did 'not believe the French or the Dutch voters rejected the European Constitution'. What he thought they rejected he did not say.

An anonymous spokescrat in Brussels simply added (presumably assuming that a second vote would naturally be forthcoming) that 'efforts will have to be made to explain things more clearly to citizens.' (He had not worked out how they would do this. In the run-up to the French vote an astonishing 45 million copies of the 852 page constitution were distributed to the French though how many got round to reading the document is unknown.)

Other bureaucrats, and some politicians, simply refused to acknowledge the significance of the overwhelming rejection of their beloved (but unpopular) constitution and, with a gloriously absurd lack of any understanding of the meaning of voting, insisted that, regardless of the fact that it had been rejected by the public the constitution would go ahead as planned. When democracy is inconvenient it must simply be brushed under the carpet. Later, all 25 EU leaders, including Blair, put their names to a joint declaration which 'noted' the results of the French and Dutch referendums, but asserted that the results 'do not call into question citizens' attachment to the Constitution of Europe.' The so-called leaders did not say how they knew this. Blair, speaking alone, claimed that 'people support the concept of the European Union'.

What the bureaucrats, and the politicians, failed to realise was that EU citizens can no longer remember why the EU was founded, they don't like what it has become and they are terrified (and disapproving) of what it is likely to be in the future.

Other EU bureaucrats slyly spoke of taking advantage of the EU's 'Declaration 30', which states that if 80% of member states ratify the new EU constitution then EU leaders can 'discuss' ways to implement the treaty anyway.

If they can't get a four-fifths majority among the countries which have voted on the constitution then there is every chance that the constitution will be broken up into chunks and adopted by the EU in little bits – regardless of the will of the people.

(Actually, even before the historic French vote, that was what was happening. Among the 'suggestions' in the EU constitution it was proposed that there should be an EU foreign minister, with his or her own diplomatic service; that criminal justice systems across Europe should be harmonised and that there should be a Charter of Fundamental Rights in addition to the Human Rights one. The bureaucrats in Brussels were so confident that they could bribe, bully or terrorise the public into allowing them to do whatever they wanted that they went ahead. They didn't wait for the result of the referendums. There is now already a new EU diplomatic corps. And there is an EU foreign minister. On the day after the French had voted 'No' to the constitution the EU foreign minister announced that EU's new diplomatic corps would continue to exist. Nor is there a hope in hell that the EU or the Labour Party will abandon the plans to harmonise Europe's criminal justice system.)

There were no signs of humility in Brussels when their constitution was rejected. No EU spokescrat had the courage to admit that they might, after all, be doing things the wrong way. The remote, arrogant and often corrupt elite who run the EU are concerned only with what they want. It does not occur to them that the public (the people who pay their bloated wages and expenses) might not want what they want.

The 'No' vote from the French was blamed on a dislike of President Chirac (who, according to some, might be in prison if he wasn't in the Elysee Palace) and a fear of what would happen to France and French culture if Turkey joined the EU. No-one working for the EU seemed to realise that the voters feel alienated from the EU – which they see as expensive, unfair, greedy, corrupt and incompetent. There is widespread dislike of the single currency, widespread belief that the European Central Bank is incompetent and widespread unhappiness at the levels of unemployment throughout Europe.

The EU is the world's most undemocratic organisation. It's very existence is built on fraud and deceit.

The EU is now such a dead duck that any English politician who claims that the EU has a future and that England's future remains within the EU is either intellectually retarded and unfit for public office or on the take and unfit for public office.

# 50

The EU has a multi-million pound fund to promote the EU constitution. And, surprise surprise, some of that money is ready to be used to campaign for a 'yes' vote if Blair's referendum on the new constitution is ever held.

So, the EU will use English money (obtained from English taxpayers) to help ensure that Britons vote the way the EU wants them to vote and that the bureaucrats get the result they want.

How bent can you get?

That's like the Blair Government using taxpayers' money to pay for a campaign to encourage electors to vote Labour at the next election.

(Perhaps I shouldn't give them ideas.)

Naturally, the EU claims that our money will be used to 'provide neutral information on the constitution and to sponsor debate'.

But does anyone really believe that?

One leading MEP has admitted that even he doesn't believe that the money will be used to promote balanced debate but will be a propaganda exercise advocating only the pro-constitution view.

## 51

When the new Iraqi constitution was being drawn up, Sir Kieran Prendergast, the UN's political affairs chief, was reported as saying that constitutions only work when there is a broad base of input and consultation.

How true.

What a pity the EU didn't follow this line of thought.

The EU constitution which Blair merrily signed in October 2004 was drawn up by a French aristocrat and a small, hand-picked team of people no-one (except perhaps their parents) has ever heard of.

## 52

The only good thing about the new EU constitution (the one even the French don't want) is that animal rights lobbyists have succeeded in ensuring that the new constitution contains a clause insisting that the rights of animals must be taken into account by the EU in all its activities.

So, if the worst comes to the worst and the dreaded new constitution becomes law, animal lovers should ensure that their governments (and the EU) obey the law.

The importance of this clause should not be under-estimated for it will mean that the EU accepts that animals have rights – and that those rights must be respected.

If the new constitution becomes law the EU will have to insist that those who farm animals, move them, kill them and turn them into food products remember and respect the animals' rights.

And it will, of course, enable campaigners to put an end to vivisection and to all types of hunting and shooting.

Animal lovers will be able to force every farmer, every

abattoir worker, every scientist, every butcher and every food conglomerate to treat the rights of animals seriously.

## 53

*'If you ask me to choose between Europe and the open sea,*
*I choose the open sea.'*
WINSTON CHURCHILL

## 54

The enlarging of the EU benefits no one as much as the European Commission itself – the little band of unelected commissars whose decisions affect our lives but who are unregulated and uncontrolled.

Back in 1960 the EU budget was around £330,000,000 a year. That was equivalent to 0.03% of the national income of the EU's member states.

By 1985 the EU budget had risen to £30,000,000,000. A total of 0.93% of the EU's gross domestic product (GDP).

And by 1998 the EU's spending money had gone up to £60,000,000,000 a year, or 1.14% of the EU's GDP.

The plans now are to increase it to 1.24% of EU GDP.

This means that the financial burden on England must rise dramatically.

The 10 countries which most recently joined the EU were mainly former members of the Soviet bloc and are, therefore, quite poor. Their entry into the EU will raise the GDP of the EU as a whole by a mere 4% overall.

But as more and more poor nations join so the enthusiasm for a rising budget will go up. Turkey is due to be the next member of the EU. Turkey will have more votes than England (it's bigger) and will doubtless want a bigger-than-ever budget.

Inevitably, therefore, existing members of the EU will have to bear most of the burden of the higher budget. And since England is one of the EU's main contributors it will be

England which will have to find the extra cash. A few more NHS hospitals will have to close and a few more motorways will have to remain unbuilt.

The plan is that by 2013 the EU will be spending £110 billion a year. Precisely what our contribution will then be is anybody's guess.

All I can tell you is that if we are still in the EU it will be a lot. A hell of a lot.

And we will all be a lot poorer than we are now.

## 55

What does the EU do with all the money it gets?

Well, half of it ends up in private bank accounts. Half of it is spent on administration. Half of it goes on huge salaries and massive expense accounts for commissioners, MEPs and bureaucrats. Half of it is wasted. Half of it is stolen. Half of it is spent promoting the EU, telling everyone what a wonderful organisation it is, designing flags and logos and indoctrinating school-children so that they grow up thinking that whatever the EU may be it is a *good thing*. And half of it is spent covering up what happens to the rest.

That's the sort of accounting we're likely to get from the EU.

The few euros which are left after the EU bureaucrats have filled their purses and wallets and safe deposit boxes, is distributed to the poorer parts of the EU. There is an EU rule that regional aid goes to areas of the EU where the income per head is less than two-thirds of the EU average. In the past some of this money has even found its way to the poorer parts of Britain. (Naturally every pound that comes from the EU comes with a good deal of EU flag waving.)

But that is about to change.

New countries which join the EU have immediate access to all the goodies. And the best goody of all is the Common Agricultural Policy which ensures that farmers get direct aid.

It is through the CAP that the EU buys up all the excess milk, butter and cereals grown within the EU. The excesses are gathered together as milk lakes and butter mountains and then, sometimes, dumped in other parts of the world. (It is this dumping of cheap food which wrecks the farming economies of developing African countries and, in the long run, leads to starvation. The EU is one of the main causes of African poverty.)

The result of the fact that poor countries are entering the EU will mean that those parts of the UK which have in the past received money from the EU (and which have, as a result, been enthusiastic supporters of the EU) are going to have to face a rather bleaker future.

Scotland, Wales, Cornwall and Merseyside have in the past received money from the EU. And the people in those areas have, not surprisingly, been firm supporters of the EU.

Oh dear.

Guess what.

Now that the EU has just had an influx of poor countries the average EU income has dropped.

Just about every region of the 10 new states will now benefit for aid.

Scotland and Wales and Merseyside can go whistle. Their days of EU money are gone. Cornwall is the only part of the UK which will still receive any EU money.

Maybe the Scots and the Welsh will now change their views about the EU.

# 56

It is difficult to see why any English politician could ever justify England's membership of the European Union. England has always been a massive contributor to the EU budget. In other words, it costs us billions of pounds a year to be members of a club which, in return for our giving it money, tells us what to do and burdens us with thousands of new laws.

It is much easier to see why other countries are wise to be members of this absurd club.

Spain, Greece and Ireland actually receive vast sums from the EU. Membership of the EU is, for example, worth around £225 for every Irish man, woman and child. And the Greeks receive around £171 a head while the Spaniards get a cash payment of £137 a head.

What is the point of being member of a club which has massive membership fees when you get absolutely nothing out of it that you want?

## 57

*'European federalists sometimes bemoan the fact that Europe's babble of different languages makes it very hard to build a common identity and to stage pan-European debates. But, when it comes to getting the EU constitution ratified, it may prove to be a distinct advantage that Europeans do not share a common language.'*
THE ECONOMIST FEB 12TH 2005

## 58

Europhilic politicians don't like giving voters a chance to air their views on the EU. Some argue that voters always have a chance to air their views at the ballot box when selecting political representatives. In Germany, governments refuse to hold referendums on the grounds that Hitler gave the voters referendums. Quite why this makes referendums unacceptable it is difficult to see. Hitler also drove around in big cars and had a mistress but this doesn't seem to have stopped EU leaders from following his example.

Besides, it is a nonsense to say that European voters have any real choices. Throughout Europe voters get very little choice. For years, none of the three main parties in England have offered any variety; all have supported the EU wholeheartedly.

And the EU disapproves sternly of parties which oppose European integration. The EU spends vast amounts of tax payers' money on making sure that the EU gets the results it wants. And parties which disapprove of the EU will soon be illegal.

## 59

*'Britain could not be an ordinary member of a federal union limited to Europe in any period which can...be foreseen.'*
WINSTON CHURCHILL

## 60

EU politicians can't tell the truth because:

- They don't know what the truth is.
- They don't care what the truth is.
- They are frightened of the truth.
- They can't control the truth.
- They don't know what the consequences are.
- Once the truth is out they know they can't put it back in the box.
- Having control of what people believe gives them power.
- If the people know the truth, they have the power.

## 61

Labour's idea of giving money to newly born children is not original. It was taken from the East German communists.

## 62

Foreign Secretary Jack Straw claimed that England had won 'each and every one' of its negotiations over the EU constitution. He claimed that supporting the EU constitution was a sign of patriotism, guaranteeing liberty, prosperity and sovereignty.

In fact, English ministers tabled 275 essential amendments to the EU constitution. They lost 248 of them.

## 63

In April 2005, Italy's Romano Prodi, former president of the EU, warned that a French rejection of the EU constitutional treaty could result in 'the fall of Europe'. He was obviously confusing the EU (a bureaucrat's delight) with Europe (a disparate collection of long established nations).

## 64

*'I wasn't born for an age like this; Was Smith? Was Jones?*
*Were you?'*
GEORGE ORWELL

## 65

Falsely forcing disparate communities to integrate will not create growth or peace or happiness. Have those who favour a United States of Europe learned nothing from the human and economic disasters of the USSR and Yugoslavia?

## 66

Supporters of the EU aren't terribly keen on democracy.

Some worry that allowing ordinary people to have a say in their future has a tendency to mess up the neatly laid plans thought up by the bureaucrats.

The fact that at least 10 of the EU's 25 member states decided to offer their citizens a vote on whether or not to accept the new EU constitution was heartily criticised by some EU stalwarts.

For example, Dietrich von Kyaw, who was Germany's

permanent representative to the EU from 1993 to 1999 complained in the EU-supporting *Financial Times* that: 'Too many national politicians, far from showing leadership, have chosen to gamble on the future of the EU, on its cohesion at a time of globalisation and of serious threats from international terrorism, failing states and nuclear proliferation.'

Er, international terrorism? Where did that come from?

Does Herr von Kyaw really think that endorsing the EU constitution would prevent terrorism? Can any human being really be that deluded?

Herr von Kyaw also said that: '...the EU needs its new constitutional treaty. But on that issue many politicians have abdicated their leadership responsibilities by turning to their electorates in order not to endanger their chances of re-election. That gives populist politicians an ideal opening to exploit ignorance and euroscepticism.'

Such arrogance and contempt for democracy would be astonishing if it were not normal among the supporters of the EU.

## 67

*'What matters is not who votes but who counts the votes.'*
STALIN

## 68

In my book *Saving England* I suggested that English electors should vote for candidates standing for small parties or standing as independents. My argument was that this would help us break the power of the big three political parties.

It's working.

At the 2005 General Election the number of people voting for independents and small parties was higher than ever.

Three independent MPs were voted in – all of them fighting on single issues which local people thought important. Who can remember the last time that happened?

George Galloway destroyed a huge Labour majority and took Bethnal Green and Bow from a sitting Labour candidate, largely by campaigning against the illegal invasion of Iraq. Peter Law stood as an independent candidate, protesting at all-women shortlists and the fact that the Labour Party had installed one of their London luvvies as the official candidate. He won dramatically with a 9,000 majority, destroying what had been one of the biggest Labour majorities in the country. And in Wyre Forest a doctor who had won the seat in 2001 on the single issue of saving the local hospital (where he had worked for 20 years) was re-elected with a massive majority.

All this shows that where voters are offered serious candidates they will vote for them and ignore the main parties.

The British National Party, which hardly received any national publicity (when it did it was derided) and whose leader had been conveniently arrested just weeks before the election, received vast numbers of votes. As did the United Kingdom Independence Party.

## 69

Overall, in the 2005 election there was a 61% turnout and Blair's Labour Party, which won, received just 21% of the electoral vote – by far the smallest mandate any English Government has ever received.

The electoral turnout was comfortably over 80% in the early 1950s. Even by the 1990s it was still well over 70%. When the Conservatives won the 1992 election there was a 78% turnout and the Tories had 33% of the electoral vote.

Since Labour came into power in 1997 people have given up voting and the electoral turn out has collapsed. In 2001 just 59% of those eligible to vote actually bothered to do so.

During the 2005 campaign, one Labour Minister memorably claimed that people no longer bother to vote because they are content with what they've got.

# 70

Has the time come to reconsider the validity and fairness of the sacred principle of 'one man one vote'?

The original concept of giving every man and woman a vote was based on the unarguably fair notion that everyone who contributes to society should have a say in how it is run.

But things have changed.

Today, it is perfectly possible for a government to get into power – and to stay there indefinitely – simply through winning the votes of people who make no contribution to society.

So many millions now receive state benefits, and are wholly dependent upon the government for their income, that a political party which is prepared to pander to them, in order to win their votes, while at the same time ignoring the needs and rights of those who work and pay tax, could stay in power for years.

I believe that Blair's Labour Party is in power because it gets votes this way. Those who voted for Labour in the last election could only have done so for entirely selfish and personal reasons. Blair and his Government have been so discredited that it is impossible to believe that anyone could have voted for them for any other reason.

And it is because they know that this is where their votes come from that the Labour Party has done nothing to stop the epidemic of benefit fraud which is destroying the welfare state. The Labour Party doesn't care two hoots that those who are genuinely in need are being pushed aside and abandoned. All the Labour Party cares about is staying in power and enjoying the perks and the money that come with the power. If this means pandering to those who prefer not to work then this is what they will do.

It is part of our electoral tradition that prisoners do not receive a vote. Why, after all, should people who do not make a positive contribution to society have a say in how society is run?

It would make just as much sense to withdraw the right to

vote from those who are long-term benefit claimants.

Our present system is ludicrous and quite unfair. It's like allowing those who receive donations from a charity to decide how the charitable contributions should be distributed and how much those who contribute to the charity should give.

Those who voted for Blair and Labour don't care about whether or not England disappears. They don't care about the dangers of global warming or genetically engineered food. They don't care how many illegal wars are started. They don't deserve a vote.

# 71

Every politician who has served in an English government since Edward Heath took England into the Common Market is a traitor. Some may not have known what was going on. They should have known. Some may now regret what they did. That doesn't alter the fact that they betrayed their country.

# 72

The Monarch has a right and a duty to advise, counsel and warn her Government. But, sadly, Queen Elizabeth II has said and done nothing to stop what is happening to her country. Despite receiving many letters from her subjects explaining how they believe they have been tricked and lied to by politicians the Queen seems amazingly happy with the fact that England is about to disappear.

Here is the standard reply sent out by the Queen to those who write and complain about the rise of the EU and the disappearance of England.

Since the reply is a 'standard' rather than a personal letter (indeed, it is more of a statement than a letter) I do not feel that it is wrong to republish it here:

*'The Queen has received your recent letter on membership of the European Union and a possible referendum on the proposed EU*

*Constitutional Treaty. As Her Majesty receives many letters on this subject, it is not possible to send an individual reply to every one.*

'*The Queen appreciates the thoughtfulness of correspondents who take the time to write and give her their views. Her Majesty follows, with interest, developments in the European Union and recognises that the United Kingdom's membership of the European Union is governed by treaties that were freely entered into, following all normal constitutional procedures.*

'*Her Majesty does have prerogative and statutory powers. However, policy on the United Kingdom's membership of the European Union is entirely a matter for The Queen's Ministers. As such, Her Majesty's own powers are exercised, by convention, on and in accordance with advice from those Ministers. As part of this important constitutional convention it is customary for Her Majesty to grant Royal Assent to Bills duly passed by Government.*

'*A copy of your letter is being forwarded to the Foreign and Commonwealth Office for the Attention of the Secretary of State for Foreign and Commonwealth Affairs.*

'*By providing my Ministers with a full list of those who write to me to complain about the EU I can help ensure that when the new Constitution has been ratified armed members of Europol will come round to your house and drag you off to a maximum security re-education facility in Poland.*'

OK I admit it. I made up the last paragraph. The rest is real.

How sad it is to have to report that it seems to me that the English people have been betrayed by Parliament, by Government and by their Monarch, Queen Elizabeth the Last.

# 73

'*My loving people, we have been persuaded by some that are careful of our safety to take heed how we commit ourselves to armed multitudes for fear of treachery, but I assure you I do not desire to live to distrust my faithful and loving people. Let tyrants fear; I have always so*

*behaved myself under God, I have placed my chiefest strength and*
*safeguard in the loyal hearts and goodwill of my subjects. And therefore*
*I am come amongst you, as you see, at this time not for my recreation*
*and disport, but being resolved in the midst and heat of battle to live*
*and die amongst you all. To lay down for God, my kingdom and for*
*my people, my honour and my blood even in the dust. I know I have the*
*body of a weak and feeble woman, but I have the heart and stomach*
*of a King and a King of England too and think it foul scorn that*
*Parma or Spain or any Prince of Europe should dare to invade the*
*borders of my realm; to which, rather than any dishonour shall grow*
*by me, I myself will take up arms, I myself will be your General,*
*Judge and Rewarder of every one of your virtues in the field. I know*
*already for your forwardness you have deserved rewards and crowns;*
*and we do assure you, on the word of a Prince,*
*they shall be duly paid you.'*
ELIZABETH I, ADDRESSING HER TROOPS WHILE AWAITING
THE ARRIVAL OF THE SPANISH ARMADA IN 1588, AND SHOWING
A RATHER MORE FEISTY DETERMINATION TO DEFEND HER
COUNTRY THAN HER NAMESAKE HAS EXHIBITED.

## 74

The Britons who have been pushing us towards Europe have
been doing so largely for personal gain. Thanks to the EU
gravy train numerous political no-hopers have become wealthy.
Greedy politicians desperate for wealth (and a chance to have
their egos massaged) have sold their country and betrayed
their heritage. There is no excuse and there can be no
forgiveness. Theirs are heinous crimes.

## 75

To celebrate the signing of the EU constitution there was a
glittering £8 million extravaganza. Well-known war criminal
Tony Blair (who signed the constitution on behalf of England)
was allowed to keep the platinum pen with which he had signed

the treaty. He, like the other signatories, was also given a goody bag, similar to those given to those who win Oscars. The goody bag included a leather document holder, a bronze statue and an expensive bottle of wine. Blair signed the constitution despite endless opinion polls which showed that the people he represented did not want him to sign.

## 76

Here is the unbiased question the French will doubtless be asked if they are invited to vote again on the EU constitution.

*'Would you like a future full of free wine, long holidays and more money than you can spend in a long and healthy life? Or do you want to reject the new EU constitution and live in pain and penury for the remainder of your short life?'*

## 77

During the 2005 English general election all three main parties completely ignored the subject of the EU and the proposed new EU constitution. They all knew that the new EU constitution was far more important for England's future than any general election and that the infamous 852 page document was an unashamed blueprint for a centralised legal system and a federal government. But the EU was the dog which didn't bark. Why so silent? Simple. All three main political parties support the EU and, although they know that the vast majority of voters want England to leave the EU, they are determined to keep us in against our will. We are now all political prisoners and the three main political parties (who should be our servants) have become our jailers.

## 78

Supporters of the EU commission want the new constitution because they say that the present system is unworkable and that a more efficient EU will be able to produce more regulations.

## 79

The Government and the EU talk constantly about the rights and the freedom which they intend to give us or to allow us. These things are not theirs to give. On the contrary, we give our authority to them solely so that they can ensure that we have the rights and the freedom to which we are entitled.

## 80

The Government's constant campaigning on behalf of the EU (frequently supported with money provided by the European Commission) is not about truth or fairness or providing information so that voters can make up their own minds. The Government's campaigning is simply about winning. And in order to win the Labour Government is prepared to lie.

Here are some of the Labour Government's recent lies about the EU:

*1. Labour claims that during the last 30 years we haven't lost any power to Brussels.*
As lies go this one is about as big as they get.

Back in 1975 when Britons were tricked into voting to stay in the Common Market we were promised that 'no important new policy can be decided in Brussels or anywhere else without the consent of an English Minister.'

That was what we were told.

Oh dear.

Today, over half the new laws which affect us come from unelected bureaucrats in Brussels. We have no opportunity to say 'No'. Most of this new legislation may, it is true, be discussed by the European Parliament, but *debating* isn't allowed in the European Parliament. And decisions are made by majority voting. Even if we say: "No, no, a thousand times no," it will make no difference. It really will be a case of "No" meaning "Yes".

*2. Labour claims that the new EU constitution (the one the French and the Dutch rejected) will make Brussels more accountable to Sovereign parliaments.*
Er, did I say the last lie was a big one? Wrong. Compared to this lie the last lie was a small one. The proposed constitution would introduce a system enabling the European commission to ignore objections from the English Parliament completely.

*3. Labour claims that the new EU constitution 'literally limits the power of the EU'.*
Another corker. They got some of the right words. But they got them in the wrong order.

In fact, the new EU constitution 'literally gives the EU unlimited powers'. The planned constitution contains a general Flexibility Clause which will enable the EU to adopt new powers which are not set out in the constitution whenever it wants to.

To accept the constitution would be like signing a contract which gave the other party the authority to revise the clauses of the contract whenever it wanted to. And gave you no power whatsoever.

It wouldn't be a bit like that. It would be exactly like that.

*4. Labour claim that the new EU constitution is a victory for England. They say that all of the Labour Government's 'red lines' were obeyed.*
Well, that's not quite exactly true.

As I have already pointed out, the Labour Government tabled a total of 275 amendments to the constitution and won 27 of them. That means that the Labour Government agreed to let the Brussels bureaucrats ignore 248 of their red lines.

Labour lost out on the creation of European Mutual Defence Pact (Blair and Co. didn't want one but there will be one); the creation of a European Foreign Minister (Blair and

Co. didn't want one but now there already is one) and a common foreign policy; common asylum and immigration systems which will mean England has no control over her borders; a provision that England must give up her seat on UN security council if the EU foreign minister wants it and the appointment of a new European Public Prosecutor.

That's five of the ones Blair and Co. lost.

They lost another 243 of those.

*5. Labour claim that we have a veto and can, therefore, say 'no' to any EU development we don't like.*
I'm not sure whether that counts as a lie or a joke.

It's so far removed from the truth that calling it a lie is like describing the sea as wet. A bit too obvious.

We gave up our veto years ago. Various Prime Ministers gave away bits of our power and Blair himself surrendered our veto in 66 areas in the two previous treaties that he signed without a referendum. Of course, it is perfectly possible that Labour hasn't noticed that yet.

I don't mind Blair signing stuff without reading it properly if he's just buying houses he can't afford, but when it comes to flogging my history I'd much prefer it if he opened his eyes occasionally.

*6. Labour say that the new constitution will result in the EU handing back some of its power to England.*
Er, oh no it won't. It doesn't say that.

At all.

Anywhere.

The EU bureaucrats will just get ever more powerful.

*7. Labour say that being in the EU has made us more prosperous.*
All together now.

'Oh, no it hasn't.'

The red tape pouring out of Brussels is destroying English industry.

The truth is that the EU (which allegedly champions free

market reform) is obsessed with legislation. And the cost of this legislation to English industry is billions a month (pounds or euros) and is rising faster than the interest debt on the Blair's posh new London house.

EU legislation is a major cause of the fact that England is now enjoying a record number of personal bankruptcies and bankruptcies among small companies.

*8. Labour claim that the EU has made Europe more peaceful.*
Just because there hasn't been a major war in Europe recently doesn't mean there isn't going to be one. The EU might as well claim credit for our fine showing in the Eurovision song contest recently.

There is only one way the EU could have made us safer.

If Blair had listened to the French instead of siding with George Bush he wouldn't have turned us into the world's No 2 terrorist target.

## 81

*'What was it that at every decisive moment made every British statesman do the wrong thing with so unerring an instinct?'*
GEORGE ORWELL (*THE LION AND THE UNICORN*)

## 82

The European Commission plans to force employers to check how hot it is each day and to gauge the strength of ultraviolet rays. If there is any risk, workers must be provided with suncream, sunglasses, a hat and a parasol (The EU has not explained who will hold a parasol over the person holding a parasol over a lollipop lady.) This is not a joke.

## 83

When (rather than if) the new EU constitution becomes law the EU will abandon all pretence that the change is cosmetic and will rush through a raft of new policies which will change Europe for ever.

+ England will cease to exist – and will become just a series of regions within the EU superstate.

+ Migrants will be given even greater rights.

+ A common education policy will be introduced – including yet more official pro-EU propaganda.

+ The amount of money available to EU bureaucrats will be massively increased.

+ The EU will have a massively increased army. Individual, national armies will disappear.

+ Far more red tape will be introduced (destroying the viability of most English companies). The number of people employed directly by the EU will rocket.

## 84

The europhiles sneer at tradition. And yet it is tradition which provides the bedrock upon which our society is built.

## 85

The people who run the EU are keen to have Turkey as a member.

Why?

Turkey is very large and very poor and will have to be given billions of pounds in aid. Turkey's gross domestic product (GDP) per head is less than a third of the average GDP in the enlarged EU. A third of all the Turks work as farmers and the cost to the EU in agricultural subsidies will be vast.

Turkey already has a population of over 70 million. It is growing much faster than Western European countries and will, within less than a generation, be the biggest member of the EU. It will then have even more votes in the European Parliament than Germany.

Those are the drawbacks.

So what's in it for the EU?

Why are our masters in Brussels so determined to bring Turkey into the EU?

Well, first and foremost the Americans want Turkey in the EU. (The Americans were effectively the founders of the EU and have long believed that a large EU is a 'good thing' for America.)

The Americans want Turkey within the EU for two reasons: first, it is partly in Europe and partly in Asia and second, it is a Muslim country. The Americans believe that if Turkey is in the EU then other Muslim countries (particularly Asian ones) will feel linked to the West. They believe that this will make it easier to 'sell' the idea of liberal, western, democracy to Muslim countries. (I didn't claim it was a logical reason. I just said it was what the Americans wanted. The Americans do not understand anything much outside Detroit.)

The EU bureaucrats, and the politicians who 'lead' Western European governments (I use the word 'lead' in a general sort of way) know that millions of Turks will move to England, France and Germany in search of higher wages. (If they come to England the Turks will, of course, go back home if they fall ill. The health care in Turkey is infinitely better than it is in England.) The idea is that the immigrating Turks will have loads of children and help solve the coming pensions crisis.

I apologise if I have given the impression that the Americans are the only stupid people around.

# 86

The EU buys sugar from European beet growers at three times the world price. Inevitably, there is massive over production of sugar within the EU. The EU deals with this by having high tariffs on imports and subsidising exports. The end result is the further impoverishment of starving people in poor countries.

## 87

A few years ago I was invited to be patron of a charity called 'Transform' which was founded to campaign towards better drug control laws. (I have, for several decades, written extensively about the benefits of decriminalising drugs which are currently illegal.) I helped the organisation as much as I could and gave them a large quantity of copies of my book *The Drugs Myth* to sell to raise funds.

Then, by chance, I discovered that my name had been taken off the charity's notepaper and web site. Puzzled both by the fact that this had happened and the fact that I had never been told I wrote to them asking for an explanation. But I never received a reply.

However, I'm pleased to report that the organisation seems to be doing well. I have discovered that it has received funding from the European Commission.

How wise they were to have removed my name as a patron. I can't believe that having the author of *England Our England* on their masthead would have done much for the charity's chances of receiving an EU grant.

## 88

The Labour Government has given the unelected Regional Assemblies complete authority over housing and planning strategies. For example, the East of England Regional Assembly has decided to build 478,000 homes in Essex, close to 600,000 which have been built since 2001. Numerous people and local bodies objected to this plan but the decision made by the Regional Assembly cannot be opposed or overturned.

Regional Assemblies are not elected bodies, they are

appointed EU quangos, made up of people who have been selected and appointed by Labour, and working directly under the guidance of the Deputy Prime Minister John Prescott.

Let me remind you again that when England disappears it will be replaced by the Regional Assemblies – which have now been set up and which are already operating and controlling our lives.

Did the Labour Party forget to mention that at the last election?

## 89

*'Individuals have a duty to violate domestic laws to prevent crimes against peace and humanity from occurring.'*
NUREMBERG WAR CRIMES TRIBUNAL 1945-6

## 90

Totalitarianism can be defined as:

1. A single mass party which is intertwined with government bureaucracy.
2. A system of terror by the police and secret police which is directed against the real and imagined enemies of the regime
3. A monopolistic control of the mass media.
4. A near monopoly of weapons.
5. A central control of the economy.
6. An elaborate ideology which covers all aspects of existence.

## 91

The British National Party (BNP) is now a signficiant political party in England.

In the general election of May 2005, the BNP and the United Kingdom Independence Party (UKIP) both fielded candidates in 76 seats. Of those 76 head-to-head contests, the BNP won 65 and UKIP won 11.

In 188 seats there was a mixture of BNP, UKIP and Veritas candidates and when the dust settled it was clear that Veritas (the party founded by former Labour MP and television personality Robert Kilroy-Silk) had received 1.46% of the vote, UKIP had 2.49% and the BNP had 4.32%.

The Green Party got a good deal more publicity than the BNP (mainly because their long-standing pro-EU policies are considered more palatable by the media) and competed head-to-head with the BNP in 31 seats. While the Greens got more of the vote in only 6 of those seats the BNP candidates got more of the vote in the other 25.

It is clear from all this that the BNP (of which, I should perhaps add, I am not and never have been either a supporter or a member) is clearly a leading British party campaigning for the rights of England and opposed to the European Union.

And yet the Labour Government has done everything it can to put the BNP out of business.

Alarmingly, Labour spokespersons have made serious attempts to stop Government employees such as policemen, school-teachers and civil servants from being members of the British National Party. After the BNP got almost 900,000 votes in the June 2004 European and local elections, Labour's Home Secretary David Blunkett (who himself subsequently resigned in disgrace after allegations that he had misused his position for personal reasons) suggested that the Government ban members of the BNP from jobs in the civil service. The wretched Blunkett, the 21st century's answer to the Witchfinder General, proposed that under a new law civil servants would have to say if they were members of the BNP (so much for the sanctity of the ballot box) and, if they were, give up either their job or their beliefs. No one in the Labour Party seems to have realised that this would have simply led to the creation of an illegal, underground party with secret members.

(This wasn't the Labour Government's only attempt to put the BNP out of business. Less than a month before the general election in 2005 the leader of the BNP was charged with race hate offences resulting from a television documentary which had been screened nine months earlier. Some thought that the arrest was timed to interrupt the political campaign of a democratic political party.)

It is difficult to think of a more totalitarian and fascist act than to ban a legal political party because you don't like it, because it is an embarrassment to the EU and because it is proving to be too successful for comfort. Indeed, deciding which political parties people can support is more than reminiscent of the old Soviet Union than of England. But in Labour's world it is, it seems, perfectly acceptable to be a supporter of a party which starts illegal wars but not acceptable to support a party which wants to defend Britain's culture and identity. The BNP has, it has been claimed, more than its fair share of thugs but if it is acceptable to ban a political party because you don't like some of the members what political party deserves to exist? The BNP's published policies are avowedly not racist. The Labour Party on the other hand, includes among its members thousands of the most obnoxious people in England and is led by a bunch of war criminals whose policies can, in my opinion, be described as fundamentally racist.

Incidentally, Labour Ministers either didn't realise or didn't care that banning membership of a political party would be a clear breach of the EU's Human Rights Act, article 10 of which (entitled Freedom of Expression) states quite clearly: 'You have the right to hold opinions and express your views on your own or in a group. This applies even if they are unpopular or disturbing. This right can only be restricted in specified circumstances (such as protecting the public health or safety, preventing crime and protecting the rights of others).'

The EU's rules and proclamations are, it seems only to be

regarded as law when they are convenient and acceptable to the EU.

## 92

EU policies have led to a rise in the success of right wing parties whose supporters object to the formation of a new European superstate.

In France, Jean-Marie Le Pen came second in the Presidential election of 2002. In Austria the Freedom Party led by Jorg Haider became part of a coalition government. (The EU said that this was unacceptable and refused to accept the Government chosen by the Austrian people.) In the Netherlands, Pim Fortuyn ran on an anti-immigration ticket in the 2002 election and was very successful until he was assassinated. In Germany the neo-Nazis made huge gains in the 2004 elections. And, of course, in England the British National Party is now the fourth most successful political party – and is rapidly gathering support.

## 93

The slogan 'Education, Education, Education', which Blair made popular when he first came to power, was actually stolen from the former East German communist regime.

## 94

The real power in the EU lies with the unelected European Commission (EC) and their bureaucratic advisers. (Recent Commissioners have included Neil Kinnock and Peter Mandelson. Need I say more?).

The European Commissioners have the exclusive right to put forward new legislation, to decide on priorities and to decide how EU members are to be integrated. Just about everything the commissioners do seems to me to be designed to guard and protect their own power, to boost the power of the EU and to speed up the rate at which the federal state is developed. All powers which are surrendered by individual nations are quickly grabbed by the EC – never to be returned.

The European Parliament exists as a rubber stamp for the EC, and to give the commission an appearance of respectability. Members of the European Parliament are there to serve the commissioners, to pass the new legislation which has been decided by the commission. Individual MEPs are allowed to speak but never for more than 90 seconds at a time.

The EU is the very antithesis of democracy; it is a perfect example of practical fascism in action. Those who support the EU do so either because they approve of the version of totalitarianism, statism and fascism purveyed by the EU or because they simply don't understand what has happened, what is happening and what is due to happen.

We are no longer in control of our lives or of our destinies. The EU is as democratic as Nazi Germany under Hitler. The police forces and prisons of individual nations now exist to support the EU.

## 95

*'Fascism has an enigmatic countenance because in it appears the most counterpoised contents. It asserts authoritarianism and organises rebellion. It fights against contemporary democracy and, on the other hand, does not believe in the restoration of any past rule.'*
JOSE ORTEGA Y GASSET (1927)

## 96

The EU is a one party state. It is a fundamentally corrupt and fascist organisation. Here are some practical examples of EU fascism in action.

The EU is introducing:

♦ Identity cards.

- Restrictions on right to trial by jury.
- The abolition of English common law.
- A dramatic increase in state surveillance.
- An ongoing war against individuality and free choice.
- A state monopoly on physical force (meaning that individuals no longer have the right to defend themselves or their property).

Like all fundamentally fascist organisations, the EU exists for the benefit of the people who run it. It is, as I've said, practical fascism in action.

## 97

The EU has always attracted and been supported by fascists. Sir Oswald Mosley, perhaps the most famous of all British fascists, an ex Labour Minister and a well-known supporter of Adolf Hitler, was very pro-EU and was active during the run up to the 1975 referendum on whether or not England should remain in the Common Market.

## 98

Nationalists, despised by the EU bureaucrats, are only concerned with preserving the ethnic and cultural identity of their own people, rather than in oppressing others.

Fascism, on the other hand, seeks to place the state above everything; above all individual or national loyalties. The aim of fascism is to subordinate everything else (including business and family life) to the state's interest

## 99

The EU, like all totalitarian, fascist or statist organisations does not approve of, or condone, free speech.

Consider, for example, what happened to Rocco Buttiglione, a traditional, conservative politician, a Professor of Moral Philosophy, who was nominated by the Italian Government as their European Commissioner but who was banned from a post as European Justice Commissioner.

Buttiglione was banned because of his traditional views on marriage and society.

Here are two of the comments he made which caused outrage within the EU:

- 'The rights of homosexuals should be defended on the same basis as the rights of all other European citizens. But I don't accept that homosexuals are a category deserving of special protection.'

- 'We have to have policies which enable women to become mothers and to develop their talents.'

For making these comments Buttiglione was portrayed as an extremist and banned as a commissioner.

He attempted to defend himself by saying that the views were private, and he apologised. But his appointment was vetoed.

The new European liberals who represent New Labour, New Europe and New Fascism, claim to be enlightened but they seem to me to be intolerant, narrow minded and bigoted.

## 100

Labour's decision to appoint Peter Mandelson as England's EU commissioner accurately sums up the Government's contempt for the electorate and their fundamental lack of moral direction. The fact that Mandelson was readily accepted as a commissioner, and seems to have fitted well into the EU bureaucracy, tells us more than we want to know about the nature of the EU. Mandelson and the EU go together well. Mandelson resigned twice in disgrace as a domestic politician. And the EU is, after all, a natural home and refuge for such politicians.

# 101

We have access to more information than any other generation. Ever. But the quality of the information, and its relevance to our needs, is of some considerable doubt. The only certainty is that a good deal of it has been deliberately distorted and manipulated and bears little resemblance to the truth. We are over-laden with information about celebrities. Our news is served up in pre-digested bite-sized chunks which have had all the goodness removed from them.

This isn't a phenomenon which is unique to England. A survey conducted in the United States of America showed that over half of American citizens have no idea where Canada is situated. You can understand them not knowing where Europe or China can be found on a map but you'd think that a few of the fat and ignorant morons might be able to find Canada. A survey in Spain (conducted just before the Spanish voted overwhelmingly to accept the ill-fated EU constitution) showed that 88% of Spaniards admitted that they knew nothing or very little about the EU and had no idea what the constitution contained or what significance it had. That didn't stop them voting for it.

But it is a phenomenon which affects us too. I suspect that an honest and properly conducted survey would show that 99% of Britons have no idea how much the EU affects their lives and just how it was mis-sold to us.

This general ignorance about crucial issues is, of course, a fault of the media. It is no accident. Part of the time they do it on purpose. And part of the time they simply cooperate and collude with the politicians who want to mislead us.

When debating the issue of vivisection many years ago (you can tell it was a long time ago because for a decade or so now vivisectors have refused to debate the issue with me in public) a leading supporter of animal experiments admitted that most animal experiments are misleading and provide false information if the results are extrapolated and applied to human patients. He admitted that he and his colleagues did not know which experiments might prove useful to doctors and which might be so misleading that they might actually be of negative benefit to doctors and patients.

I pointed out that if the experimenters themselves don't know which experiments are valid, and can be relied upon, then all experiments are useless. If you have 10 pieces of information and know that six of those pieces of information are inaccurate and that four are accurate – but don't know which six are bad and which four are good – then all 10 pieces of information are useless and aren't worth the effort of obtaining them.

The same is true of the information you obtain from newspapers, from television and from the radio.

So much of the information available to us is biased, prejudiced, bent and planted that it is nigh on impossible to determine which information is of value and which is not.

This is true of almost all so-called 'news' but it is particularly true of 'news' about the European Union.

As a general rule you can rely on the fact that any information about the EU which you obtain from a newspaper, a television station or a radio station is worthless. This is, of course, particularly true of information provided by the BBC which is I believe, as a purveyor of news, infinitely untrustworthy and infinitely unreliable. In my opinion, of course.

## 102

The Government can spend as much public money as it likes explaining its policies – and extolling the virtues of the European Union. For example, the Government spent £30 million of taxpayers' money on its euro information campaign, though they never did get round to having a referendum on whether or not we would join the euro. The European Commission, based in Brussels, has a virtually bottomless purse. It can spend as much of our money as it likes telling us that the EU is wonderful, essential, valuable and crucial to our future good health, well-being, security and financial stability. Opposition to the EU sometimes seems to be pretty much limited to the advertising budget of Publishing House (the publishers of *England Our England*, *Saving England* and this book).

# 103

I have lost count of the number of broadcasters and publications which have banned me – or tried to censor my work. It was partly to ensure that my books get published without being censored that I started publishing the initial editions myself. (And then selling subsequent foreign rights to other publishers.)

But I'm now also rapidly losing count of the number of publications which have banned *advertisements* for my books.

Some of the bans are, to say the least, surprising.

*The Spectator* (which you might think of as a rather free thinking magazine with an affection for original thought and controversy) has banned advertisements for all my books. The editor seems to have been particularly upset by my books *Rogue Nation* and *England Our England* though I gather that his distress only developed after some of his readers threatened to cancel their subscriptions if he continued to allow me to buy advertising in the magazine. *The Spectator* describes itself as 'informative, irreverent, controversial and intelligent' and claims that it 'comprises an elegant, liberating mix of politics, current affairs, literature and the arts'. It seems, however, that the magazine doesn't like too much of a mix and doesn't want to be liberating all the time. *The Spectator* has refused to run any Publishing House advertisements. It is difficult to imagine a more brutal and heavy-handed form of censorship. *The Spectator* says it is banning our ads because the magazine 'received so many letters of complaint, and threats to cancel subscriptions...'. An allegedly political publication which shies away from anything criticising America, the EU or the pharmaceutical and medical industries because of readers' complaints really ought to turn itself into a gardening magazine.

A magazine called *Best of British*, which rather sounds as if it should be full of patriotic fervour, banned the insert advertisement for *England Our England* shortly after accepting it. (They sent back a lorry load of inserts which had been specially printed to be included in the magazine.) If you're a subscriber or reader of *Best of British* you might like to think again and spend your money elsewhere. They aren't alone. A surprisingly long list of magazines have banned advertisements for my books. And *England Our England* is the book they seem most keen to ban.

A magazine called *The Dalesman* has banned advertisements for *England Our England*. Huge publishing giant IPC banned advertisements for *England Our England* from all their magazines. And advertisements for the same book have been banned from the magazine published by the National Trust.

Astonishingly, I'm told that even a magazine published by the Council for the Preservation of Rural England has banned an advert for *England Our England*.

Since England (rural or otherwise) won't even exist unless we all fight hard to save it, how could the Council for the Preservation of Rural England do this? How can an organisation which promotes itself as protecting England ban an advert for a book which is intended to keep England alive? An organisation called English Heritage has also banned advertisements for *England Our England*. And at least one magazine which is circulated to former war veterans has refused further advertisements because of the number of complaints received from its readers. If the EU is allowed to do what it wants to do, the Second World War will have been a complete waste of time and those who died will have done so in vain. How can any war veteran possibly complain that it is racist to attempt to defend England?

(Incidentally, hundreds of review copies of *England Our England* and *Saving England* were sent out to national and regional newspapers and magazines. Virtually every publication refused to review or mention the books.)

*England Our England* has, I think, been banned more than any other book of mine.

Why do so many publications ban adverts for my books?

It is, I suppose, impossible to generalise. (Though it is worth making the point that not one publication has refused to carry advertisements because they have found a factual error in a book.)

My books do question Government policies, do pose a real threat to many parts of the Establishment and are a commercial threat to many multinationals. And that, it seems, is what frightens so many editors.

I suspect that an editor who once refused to take any more of my articles might have the answer.

'We can't print your work,' he told me, without any embarrassment, 'because you make people think.'

Curious.

I always thought that was one of an author's main responsibilities.

I hope my books continue to make people think.

Magazines, newspapers and broadcasters may ban them.

But I'll continue to write them.

And they will continue to be published until we run out of breath or money.

## 104

The English press has, by and large, remained pathetically and inexplicably loyal to the European Union. I don't think any newspaper has remained more absurdly loyal than the *Financial Times*. On the 3rd June 2005, the same week that the people of France and Holland had dramatically and clearly rejected the new EU constitution (and, indeed, made it clear that they didn't have much enthusiasm for the EU either) the *Financial Times* made an extraordinary attempt to defend the EU.

'...the EU has become a victim of its own success,' the newspaper argued. 'War has receded into the distant memory – in western Europe at least – and means little to two generations. Meanwhile, the economic prosperity and comfortable lifestyles of Europe's social model, under pinned by the EU's single market, have already been banked by Europe's citizens.'

So, according to the *Financial Times*, the people of Europe rejected the EU's proposed constitution because the EU has been too successful.

Such arrogance and ignorance almost beggars belief.

Does the *FT* really not know that unemployment levels in Europe are now between 10% and 15% (in England they are lower only because the Government has fiddled the figures)? Does the *FT* really regard the euro as a success? Does the *FT* genuinely believe that the Common Agricultural Policy is successful and sensible? Does the *FT* approve of the activities of the European Central Bank? Or does the *FT* simply feel obliged (for some reason of which I am not aware) to support the EU and to search for explanations and excuses for its obvious unpopularity?

## 105

Anyone who relies on mainstream newspapers, television or radio for news about the EU will have a very superficial and one-sided view of what is going on. What masquerades as news is simply a mixture of lies, half truths, spin, counterspin and propaganda. The aim of the media today is to misinform, to manipulate and to make you afraid.

Quite rightly, distrust of the press is becoming widespread.

A major recent survey in the USA showed that 45% of Americans believe little or nothing that they read in newspapers. Twenty years ago only 16% of readers expressed such profound scepticism.

Apart from newsletters and small publishers there is no free press in America.

And with the exception of newsletters and small publishers there is no free press in England either.

In most countries where there is no free press it is because their governments have used brute force to censor the media. Tyrants from the dusty depths of history right up to the Nazis and the communists knew the importance of controlling the press.

But things are different now. They're worse.

The difference with the 21st century despots is that they know how to manipulate the media and, instead of just dipping journalists in boiling tar, they hire tame journalists to spread their message. Labour's spin doctors were, in a spiritual sense, fathered by Hitler and Goebels.

Today, politicians may not own the media and they may no longer need to chop off the arms and heads of troublesome scribes, but they can control the media with ever increasing subtlety. News used to be defined as things someone didn't want to see in print – these days it's the opposite; it's stuff someone in power *wants* you to read.

The result is that although we may *seem* to have a free press, we don't. And that's worse than having a despot who boils disobedient journalists in oil. What you read in your newspaper and what you see on television and what you hear on the radio are, by and large, the accepted messages. People believe what they see and what they hear and what they read.

But today's journalists are muzzled not by the threat of violence but by the promise of wealth and fame and success. The statist elite of the EU and Labour don't kill journalists – they buy them.

Today's journalists have given up their spirit in return for money, fame and honours. Journalists used to pride themselves on their freedom and independence. Today's journalists are servile, weak and greedy. They are also easily bribed.

The people who should be protecting our freedom are helping our tyrannical rulers take it from us. The rulers tell the journalists that what they are doing is 'inevitable' and 'necessary' and they talk of threats from terrorism and the need for progress.

Today's journalists have no sense of history and no ability to think for themselves; they have become part of show business. Most are not in the slightest bit interested in truth. They will blow whichever way the wind takes them.

Journalists and editors have chosen popularity with their bosses, gold and fame, above principle. They want to be 'in' with the 'in crowd', they want to be liked. They are sycophantic quislings not journalists. They grovel at the feet of third rate politicians and businessmen and they suppress the truth for an invitation to Chequers and a company car (preferably with chauffeur).

It is the role of journalists to harry, criticise and question politicians. Always. Whoever is in power. Journalists should never have friends among politicians and should never accept favours. It is as bad for a journalist to accept hospitality from a politician as it would be to accept a bribe from an industrialist.

But among the 300 guests officially entertained, at taxpayers' expense, by the Blairs during Labour's first term in power between 1997 and 2001 were (in addition to an Italian nobleman and his wife and two daughters, who had loaned the Blairs their Tuscan villa for a holiday) a clutch of well-known journalists.

Now, if any of those journalists had been writing a story, say, on the oil industry and had spent a weekend dining and wining at the expense of an oil company chief do you not think there might have been raised eyebrows?

When employees of the BBC accept such an invitation, and the BBC seems unperturbed by their accepting it, serious questions should be asked about the independence of the whole organisation. Journalists should avoid the hospitality of the people they are supposed to be investigating as determinedly as they should (but don't) refuse honours or awards or prizes. Any journalist who accepts a peerage, a knighthood or even an MBE has betrayed his readers. Dammit, journalists shouldn't even be on first name terms with the people they write or broadcast about. They shouldn't eat with them or drink with them.

Niccolo Machiavelli recommended that a Prince could make someone a puppet by 'dignifying him, enriching him, binding him to himself by benefits, and sharing with him the honours...of the State.'

He was right.

What all this means is that those who rely upon the press and upon TV and radio for their news, and for an interpretation of the news, will be unable to see what is happening or form useful judgements.

You cannot possibly rely upon your daily newspaper or news programme for anything approaching the truth about the EU. Indeed, I would go further. Every time you read an article praising the EU in a national newspaper you should assume that the writer is lying. And every time you listen to a laudatory programme about the EU on any BBC station I think you should ask yourself not whether the broadcaster is telling the truth but why he might be lying.

## 106

It has long been clear to me that the BBC is a very biased broadcasting organisation, which takes a strong pro-establishment line on almost every issue.

I used to work for the BBC regularly – presenting

programmes on both radio and television. But I don't get invited to appear much on the BBC these days. Review copies of my books are sent to programme editors and presenters but, on the whole, we would get as much response if we sent copies to the Man in the Moon. When representatives of the BBC do ring up it is usually to appear on something in which I have absolutely no interest, and which is unlikely to give me any opportunity to embarrass any part of the official establishment. A little while ago, for example, I received a message offering me a fee of £2,000 of licence payers' money to appear on a 'celebrity' issue of a BBC quiz programme. (I declined.) I rather doubt, however, that I will be invited to discuss this book on any BBC programme.

The BBC seems to me to support the medical establishment, the meat industry and the drug industry and to say that it is not keen to give air time to my views on doctors or the health service, or to my views on the pointlessness of animal experimentation, is something of an under-statement. I have never heard a BBC programme (on radio or television) which was fair to pro-animal campaigners, that dealt with the EU fairly, that dared to criticise American Imperialism with gusto or that criticised doctors and drug companies. The BBC usually only gives air time to politicians and other establishment figures and gives little (or preferably no) time to anyone threatening the establishment with contrary or original thoughts. Not for nothing is the BBC known not as the British Broadcasting Corporation but as the Blair Broadcasting Corporation, the Bush and Blair Chorus and the Bent Broadcasting Corporation. The whole organisation spins more than a top. After watching a BBC news programme I feel dizzy from all the spinning.

It has, for some time now, also been pretty clear to me that the BBC does not like to broadcast uncomfortably trenchant criticism of the European Union. My book *England Our England* is probably the biggest selling book on politics to have been published in England in recent years. And yet I have discussed it just once on the BBC, on a late night local radio programme. (The presenter later reported an unprecedented interest in the broadcast.)

I am not the only person to have noticed that the BBC takes an unusually partisan line on the EU. This pro-European bias has been evident to many listeners for many years and few people were surprised when, in June 2004, a study conducted by the Centre for Policy Studies revealed that the BBC gave twice as much coverage to pro-EU speakers as to eurosceptics. (I'd like to see, but am unlikely ever to obtain, a list of whatever direct and indirect grants and financial inducements the BBC may have received from the European Union.)

Naturally, representatives of the BBC are invariably quick to defend their organisation. I suspect that some of them really believe that they are impartial and it is certainly a fact that they often fail to realise just how much their bias is showing. People who work for the BBC don't think of themselves as being part of the establishment (in fact many of them like to think of themselves as being rather radical) but with the possible exception of the British Medical Association I don't think I've ever known a more pro-establishment body than the BBC. The BBC has a hierarchy based on the civil service and certainly doesn't reflect the diversity of opinion in England. Very few BBC employees have ever experienced life in the free market (the ones who have, have often failed).

The problem is that the BBC's internal environment, their in-house culture, is terribly biased towards Labour and all its best-established enthusiasms. I believe that any honest broadcaster would have left the BBC in disgust years ago. The European Union is important to Labour and so it is important to the BBC too. (The BBC's uncomfortable, and for it rather embarrassing, position over the illegal invasion of Iraq was merely a reflection of the Labour Party's own internal schism.)

Most BBC staff members are recruited through advertisements which appear exclusively in left-wing pro-Labour newspapers such as the *Guardian* and the organisation grows and grooms its own managers instead of recruiting from outside. Inevitably, many of the people who work for the BBC are *Guardian* readers. There are uncomfortable and unacceptable links between BBC staff and the Labour Party. One BBC presenter and her company are alleged to have received £600,000 in public money since Labour took over the government. Would anyone trust a journalist reporting on, say, the drug industry who earned part of their income working for the drug industry?

Is it really surprising, therefore, that the BBC ends up supporting the EU and refusing to allow the critics of the EU fair access to its airtime? Is it surprising that BBC staff invariably seem frightened of producing anything likely to upset the establishment? Was it really surprising when one well-known presenter referred to the Labour Party as 'we'? Most BBC staff may not be stupid enough to endorse one party but they don't even realise that their prejudices are prejudices. They simply regard their views as 'right'.

In my view, the BBC produces very little real investigative journalism and no consumer protection. The organisation is plump, complacent and infinitely pro-establishment; full of people who are terribly pleased with themselves and scared witless that their comfy sinecure may end. Is it any wonder that young BBC broadcasters seem to do nothing original or daring or likely to upset any part of the establishment within and without the BBC, unless it is acceptably original or daring (in which case of course it is neither).

The ultimate insult, of course, is that it is impossible to listen to the radio or watch television in England without paying a hefty annual fee to the BBC. Where else in the world do the citizens have to pay to be indoctrinated? Does no one outside the BBC realise that any broadcaster which is totally dependent upon the establishment and the government of the day for its very existence must end up as no more than a tool for both.

Although the BBC gets its income from a tax on the public (whether they watch its programmes or not) the BBC is effectively a state owned broadcaster. It certainly acts like one. No one with a brain would expect to turn on the BBC to listen to the news. The BBC is a good old-fashioned state broadcaster. It would have been comfortable operating in the USSR in the 1960s.

## 107

*'The most consistent and ultimately damaging failure of political journalism in America has its roots in the clubby/cocktail personal relationships that inevitably develop between politicians and journalists. When professional antagonists become after-hours drinking buddies, they are not likely to turn each other in.'*
HUNTER S. THOMPSON
(*FEAR AND LOATHING ON THE CAMPAIGN TRAIL*)

## 108

You cannot believe anything you read or hear about the EU. Question everything. Including me. And this book.

But think about this: the people promoting the EU do so for power and money. What do I have to gain?

If I just wanted to sell books and make money I could apply for, and doubtless obtain, a large EU grant. I could, I suspect, arrange for the EU to purchase thousands of copies of such a book to give away. A book extolling the virtues of the EU would probably prove enormously profitable without needing to sell a single copy.

On the other hand, this book, written from the heart, will be difficult to sell. Huge publishing groups will refuse to take advertisements for it. Newspapers and broadcasters will refuse to review it or promote it.

Why on earth would I write and publish such a book if the facts weren't true and I didn't believe wholeheartedly in the message?

# 109

I did very few interviews for *England Our England*. Most broadcasting companies refused even to mention the book. On one rare and memorable occasion when I was interviewed on a national radio station the presenter became so irate in defence of the EU, so aghast that anyone could dare question its existence, and so furious that he could not disprove any of the arguments in the book, that he suddenly cut the interview short and announced that he was going to refuse to mention the title of the book.

He was, presumably, worried that his more curious listeners might find a copy of the book, read it and discover the truth.

# 110

I have received a constant hailstorm of mail from readers (mostly anonymous and capable only of flirting with literacy) writing to complain about my book *England Our England*. Some claim that the EU is wonderful. They all quote documents published by the Government and the EU showing how marvellous the EU is. They seem blissfully unaware that the EU is a celebration only of corruption and a monument only to political vanity and greed.

Most surprising of all, perhaps, has been the storm of scrawled messages accusing me of being 'racist' and 'fascist'. Naturally, none of those who have written in this way had actually read the book (I rather doubt if they would have been capable even if they had been willing) and so none were aware that the word 'fascist' describes, quite perfectly, the activities of the European Union and its supporters. I would have written back to remind them that Sir Oswald Mosley was one of the most fervent early supporters of the EU had I been confident that they would have known who he was. I would have liked also to have pointed out to them that whereas it is most certainly racist to oppress those of a particular race (the English) it is equally certainly not 'racist' to attempt to defend the culture, history, identity and existence of England. Unfortunately, it is not possible to have much of a dialogue with EU supporters. Most write only in capital letters (using liberal quantities of red and green ink) and the ones who remember to give their names invariably forget to include their addresses.

# 111

I will, I have no doubt, receive a good many letters from readers wanting to know why I haven't included references for all the items in this book.

Good question.

But the answer is just as good.

The truth is, dear reader, that I have a room full of papers, documents, letters, books, cuttings, journals, magazines and other research material.

If I included a full list of references the result would be that the book would be twice as thick. It would, therefore, cost a good deal more to print and to post. Very few people would want to buy it. And the message would remain largely unread.

I had to choose between writing a fully referenced book to be read by a very small number of people and writing a more reasonably priced, more accessible book designed to be read by as large number of people as possible.

What do you think would be most likely to make a real difference?

That's what I thought.

## 112

The EU is developing a long-term strategy to address factors which it (i.e. the bureaucrats who make up EU policy) believes may contribute either to 'radicalisation' or to 'recruitment for terrorist activities'.

I have no idea precisely what this means in practice, but it seems clear that publications and other media productions which threaten the EU will soon be under threat.

## 113

Can there be anyone left who doesn't believe that modern, Western Governments now routinely use 'fear' to persuade us to accept their oppressive new laws?

In England, where Blair and his bunch of fascist cronies now run the country as though they own it, the Government has become outrageously, uncaringly arrogant in its use of fear as a weapon to control the voters.

For example, on the evening of November 22nd 2004 the ITN 10.30pm news led with a story about how England's security forces had thwarted a plot to fly hi-jacked aeroplanes into Canary Wharf and Heathrow airport.

Was anyone arrested? Er, it appears not.

Were any planes actually hi-jacked? Er, apparently not.

Did anything actually happen? Er no.

Is there any evidence at all for this preposterous claim? Well, just that a Government source said there could have been an attack if they hadn't stopped it.

And that's it.

So why did the Government want to scare us all half to death on November 22nd?

Could it possibly be because on November 23rd, the day after releasing this blatant 'scare story', the Government revealed its plans to introduce yet more fascist and intrusive laws, giving the State ever increasing powers over us and taking away the last remnants of our privacy and our liberty?

The Government clearly thinks all voters are stupid.

And so, it seems, do the various branches of the media.

My advice is simple: don't believe anything any politician ever says and don't believe anything published or broadcast by the mass media.

Question everything. (Naturally, I expect you to question everything I write too.) Turn up your scepticism to full power. Constantly ask yourself 'Why? Who gains from this news item?'

# 114

Britons are going to have to carry ID cards if we remain in the EU. Even though compulsory ID cards are almost certainly a breach of the Human Rights Act. It is EU policy. The Italian Government, for example, has stated that ID cards will strengthen 'the feeling of unity within the EU'. (We will, presumably, all have matching EU ID cards in the same way that we now all have matching EU passports.)

The EU is demanding 'harmonised solutions' on biometric identification and data. In practical terms this means that the bureaucrats in Brussels are demanding an EU-wide population register and ID cards. It is demanding national ID cards which will be used to store health, school and benefit records. Each card will carry either the fingerprints of the owner or an iris scan and a European identity register will be set up. There will be biometric readers in doctors' surgeries and in hospitals. (It will be impossible to get treatment without your card being scanned.) Oddly enough, the Labour Party suddenly became keen on ID cards at the same time as the bureaucrats in Brussels said that they had to be issued. (As is often the case English politicians are reluctant to admit that ideas like this come from Brussels. There are two reasons for their reluctance: first, they know that the public will be even more unwilling to accept the proposal and second they don't like to admit just how little power they have.)

To begin with, individual countries arranged to satisfy the EU's requirements in their own ways.

Back in 1994, when it was announced that England would be introducing new pictorial driving licences from July 1996, it was denied that this was an infringement of personal liberty. The Government did, however, admit that it was planning to include one or two other bits of information on the driving licences. When pressed for details the Government admitted that driving licences would include a computer chip which would contain: details of the driver's next of kin, address, occupation, place of employment, all previous driving details (including court appearances), insurance details, blood group, fingerprints, medical details, retinal pattern, DNA profile and national insurance number. All this information would, of course, be available to Government employees and to anyone else equipped with the requisite scanner and, of course, to anyone prepared to pay for it. In addition, it was acknowledged that the photographs on driving licences would be readable by surveillance cameras installed to track the movements of cars and their occupants around England. ID cards are heaven sent for a fascist organisation like the EU. They will enable the EU to spy on us and to make money. Your personal financial and medical records will be readily available to all Government employees. Your tax inspector will know what illnesses you have had, and the receptionist at your local medical centre will know how much you earn and how much tax you pay. Every few years we will all have to line up at identity registration centres to be fingerprinted or to have our eyeballs scanned. We will have to be fingerprinted again if we want to buy a house or register with a doctor. (Is there any evidence that the eyeball scans they are planning to use are safe and won't make us blind?) Our movements are already tracked by cameras in the streets and on the roads. (Cameras which are allegedly there to prevent crime but which have yet to be shown to have prevented any crimes at all.) We will soon have 'black boxes' in our cars which will enable the EU to track our journeys mile by mile (in case our progress is missed by the cameras) and many Government employees are being fitted with hidden microphones disguised as name badges to record our conversations.

It is clear, in retrospect, that the driving licence was the precursor of the ID card which the Labour Government is now determined to force us to carry. This was, remember, 1994 – some years before September 11th 2001. There was no mention of the need to introduce ID cards to combat terrorism. Nor indeed, were these early ID cards promoted (as Blair did in May 2005) as a method of combating identity theft.

It is important to remember that ID cards (similar to those which will be introduced throughout Europe) were introduced in Germany under Hitler (and had to be available at all times for inspection by the police). And ID cards were introduced in the USSR under Stalin. They were required for internal travel.

The new ID cards proposed by Blair and the EU are also similar to, but more intrusive than, the identity cards which were utilised in South Africa some years ago. The South African identity cards stated the name of the bearer and where he came from. If the police stopped anyone he had to show his identity card. If he was in an area prohibited to him he could be arrested. If he didn't have his card he could be arrested. If arrested he would be taken to a police station and interrogated and perhaps imprisoned. The people who suffered most from these laws were quiet, decent, law-abiding folk who were trying to go about their normal daily business. Those who were not quiet, decent and law-abiding rarely got stopped by the police. They moved around quietly, keeping a good look out and making a quick getaway if spotted. The police, largely being bullies and cowards, much preferred to harass normal, law-abiding citizens rather than chase the genuine bad guys.

If the EU and Blair have their way we will all have to carry our ID cards at all times. If stopped and asked for identification we will have to show our cards. We will be arrested if we dare go out without our cards. ID cards will be used to enable the authorities to find, imprison and exterminate those who cause too much trouble (such as writing books like this one).

And, remember, our cards will contain far, far more information than the cards which were used in South Africa or Nazi Germany. The KGB and the Stasi would have loved ID cards like these. The information on our compulsory cards will be passed to MI5 and MI6.

There will, in future, be many new offences relating to ID cards. It will, for example, be a criminal offence not to tell the authorities if your card (which you will have paid for) has been damaged or does not work properly. It will be a criminal offence to fail to tell the authorities of any change in your personal circumstances. Remember, there has never been any serious public debate about this fascist surveillance system which is supported only by fascist bureaucrats and by businesses which will make billions out of supplying the cards and out of the information they will be able to extract from them.

I don't believe anyone seriously believes that ID cards will stop crime or terrorism. Anyone in a position of authority who genuinely believes that should be relieved of his or her post immediately, led away quietly and placed in a padded room where they can sit quietly, avoiding bright lights and noises. Spain has ID cards but these did not prevent the Madrid bombings. The September 11, 2001 hijackers all travelled on legitimate papers. And the introduction of ID cards will most certainly not improve the security of individual citizens in any way. The more people who have access to your personal information, the greater the risk of you being a victim of identity theft. The actions of the EU and the Government will positively *encourage* identity theft. The incidence of identity theft has already increased dramatically as the amount of information demanded from individuals by the authorities has increased. Every time personal information is put into the public domain the security of the individual diminishes. ID cards will make life worse – and infinitely more dangerous – for all of us.

There are a good many questions about ID cards which remain unanswered. (Indeed, apart from me, no one seems to be asking the questions.) What will happen when people lose their ID cards? What happens when they are stolen? How do you go about getting a new one when you move house or change your name or job? The EU says that we will need to produce our ID cards when opening bank accounts. But most new bank accounts are opened over the Internet. Does this mean that we are expected to entrust our ID cards to the mail?

The extent of the risk to our personal security is perhaps best exemplified by the rise in personal identity theft which has taken place recently. Identity theft is currently estimated to cost American consumers more than $50 billion a year and it is a problem which is rapidly spreading in Europe.

There are, without doubt, two simple reasons for this.

First, a vast amount of personal, confidential information is now floating around in banks and public offices. The introduction of ID cards will simply increase this phenomenon.

Second, the people with whom we are forced to share our private and confidential information do not seem to regard it, once they've got it, as private or confidential. They certainly don't seem to take a great deal of care with it. The *Financial Times* reported in autumn 2004 that fewer than a quarter of computers disposed of by companies have been properly cleansed of their data. Of 350 leading companies interviewed 75% had recently sold or given away unwanted computers but only 23% had wiped the memories sufficiently to make the data on them unrecoverable. The companies who were interviewed included leading financial organisations which hold sensitive customer information and have a legal requirement to ensure that it remains confidential. It is important to remember that if hackers obtain your fingerprints or iris scans from a bank's computer or web site then your private biometric data could be permanently in the hands of criminals.

The Bank of America is reported to have 'lost' computer tapes containing the personal data of 1.2 million American Government employees. A data collection company called ChoicePoint revealed that criminals had gained access to the social security numbers, addresses and other personal data of hundreds of thousands of people. A fraud ring had infiltrated the company (which said it maintained strict security standards). One of ChoicePoint's rivals then followed suit, revealing that 'unauthorised users' had compromised the identities of 310,000 of its customers. A shoe retailer admitted that its stores' credit card data had been breached. The US Secret Service said that at least 100,000 valuable numbers had been accessed. Later it turned out that the number of credit card holders whose security had been breached was, in fact, 1.4 million. By June 2005 it was estimated that the financial details, health records and social security numbers of 50 million Americans had been made available to criminals.

Banks and insurance companies and government bodies constantly demand and accumulate personal information. It only needs one crook working in a bank or government office to make thousands of people vulnerable to identity theft. Can the big banks really assure us that they never have disgruntled or greedy employees?

The only people who will benefit from ID cards will be

those running large corporations which can buy our personal information from the Government and use it to target us more accurately and those running the Government who will have more power over us. (Although I forecast several years ago that the Government would sell this information, the Government only confirmed this in June 2005 when a spokesman eventually admitted that it would allow commercial companies to tap into its database and extract private, personal information about all citizens.)

There is a finite amount of power in the world: as they get more power so we get less.

## 115

'If you don't have anything to hide, why would you object to carrying an ID card?' asked an acquaintance.

'Tell me your income, your bank account number, what diseases you have had, when you last went to see the doctor, your home address, all your telephone numbers, your PIN numbers and your passwords.'

'No!' he answered, clearly rather offended.

'Why not?'

'Those are private. I'm not telling you stuff like that.'

'If the EU gets its way and forces us all to carry ID cards I will be able to *buy* all your private and confidential information. And every EU and Government employee will have access to all your personal information.'

## 116

Terrorists visiting England won't have to have biometric passports. But, thanks to the EU, Englishmen and Englishwomen will need to have them if they want to re-enter their own country.

## 117

The environment the EU and the Government have created is tailor-made for crooks. In April 2005 the Inland Revenue had to warn people to be aware of bogus letters sent on Revenue headed notepaper and allegedly from the Inland Revenue Central Tax Unit asking for private personal and financial details. How many people would dare say 'No' to a request purporting to come from the Inland Revenue?

## 118

*'Above all, the European Economic Community takes away Britain's freedom to follow the sort of economic policies we need.'*
TONY BLAIR, WRITING IN HIS PERSONAL MANIFESTO
WHEN STANDING FOR PARLIAMENT IN BEACONSFIELD IN 1982

*'We'll negotiate a withdrawal from the EEC which has drained our natural resources and destroyed jobs.'*
TONY BLAIR, PLEDGING HIS OPPOSITION TO THE EEC
WHEN STANDING FOR PARLIAMENT IN SEDGEFIELD IN 1983

*'On the day we remember the legend that St. George slayed a dragon to protect England, some would argue that there is another dragon to be slayed: Europe.'*
TONY BLAIR, IN PATRIOTIC AND STANDARD
VOTE-WINNING MOOD ON ST. GEORGE'S DAY 1997, IN AN
INTERVIEW WITH *THE SUN* NEWSPAPER

*'I am a passionate pro-European. I always have been.'*
TONY BLAIR, SPEAKING TO THE EU IN 2005

## 119

Changing the way we think about one another, and encouraging suspicion and fear, don't do much for our comfort and security.

I have on my desk this letter from a reader in Lancashire:
*Dear Dr Coleman*
*A man has just moved into a house across the road from us. He lives on his own and hardly speaks to anyone. However, the other day I was watching when he had a computer delivered. Should I inform the police in case he may be a paedophile?*

## 120

Adolf Hitler passed an Enabling Law, which gave him the power to issue laws without the approval of the Reichstag. He was entitled to do this even where the proposed new laws deviated from the constitution. The Enabling Law licensed the Nazis to act as they saw fit and gave total authority to the Führer. Both Bush and Blair have passed similar laws.

## 121

'*A nation can survive its fools and even the ambitious. But it cannot survive treason from within. An enemy at the gate is less formidable, for he is known but the traitor moves among those within the gates freely, his sly whispers rustling through all the alleys, heard in the very halls of government itself. For the traitor appears not as a traitor; he speaks in the accents familiar to his victims, and he wears their face and their garments, and he appeals to the baseness that lies deep in the hearts of all men. He rots the soul of a nation; he works secretly and unknown into the night to undermine the pillars of the city; he infects the body politic so that it can no longer resist. A murderer is less to be feared.'*
CICERO (106 BC – 43 BC)

## 122

Blair's main ambition is, it seems, to create a legacy; to be remembered as a Great Man. He is particularly proud of his role in integrating England further into the EU. Some would see such work as traitorous; nothing more than simple treachery. But Blair sees it as creating for himself a place in history.

Blair will be remembered.

But he won't be remembered for his attempts to destroy our culture and history. The EU won't last long.

Blair will be remembered as a war criminal. Stalin, Hitler, Mussolini, Bush and Blair. A quintet of the world's most evil men.

## 123

A Prime Minister who will take the country to war on a lie, and who will steadfastly refuse to apologise when the whole country knows that he is a war criminal and a liar, will not tell the truth about the EU.

## 124

What's the difference between Adolf Hitler and Tony Blair?
All I can think of is the moustache.

## 125

*'It would have been quite impossible for us to develop our plan for the world if we had been subjected to the lights of publicity during those years. But, the world is more sophisticated and prepared to march towards a world government. The supra-national sovereignty of an intellectual elite and world bankers is surely preferable to the national autodetermination practised in past centuries.'*
DAVID ROCKEFELLER, BILDERBERG CLUB
PERMANENT MEMBER, (1991)

## 126

The 'Big Brother' rules so beloved by the European Union and the Labour Party are 'sold' to us on the basis that they are essential for catching terrorists. This is, to put it politely, a bare-faced lie. Big Brother rules (such as banks demanding copies of passports and the Government threatening to introduce identity cards) punish everyone and catch no one. Money is wasted and nothing is achieved – apart from the loss of our liberty and the increase of identity theft.

Does anyone in Brussels or Whitehall really, really believe that terrorists will be thwarted by being unable to open bank accounts unless they provide two recent gas bills? Does any bureaucrat anywhere genuinely believe that terrorists will halt their activities if it becomes illegal to go for a walk in the park without an ID card in your pocket?

If anyone believes that, they should be certified insane.

## 127

We want our country back.

## 128

*'(People) more readily fall victims to the big lie than the small lie, since it would never come into their heads to fabricate colossal untruths, and they would not believe that others could have the impudence to distort the truth so infamously.'*
ADOLF HITLER, IN *MEIN KAMPF*

## 129

In addition to his view about the size of a lie being important, Hitler also believed that if a lie was repeated often enough it would, eventually, be confused with the truth by the greater part of the population.

## 130

In 1941, Walter Funk, Hitler's economics Minister, launched the Europaische Wirtschafts Gemeinschaft (European

Economic Community) to establish a single European currency – the reichsmark. Hitler's plan was to integrate the European economy into a single market.

In 1945, Hitler's Masterplan (captured by the Allies) included a scheme to create an economic integration of Europe and to found a European Union on a federal basis. The Nazi plan for a federal Europe was based on Lenin's belief that: 'Federation is a transitional form towards complete union of all nations.'

I will send a bottle of good champagne to the first person who can define a noticeable difference between the design of Hitler's planned EU and the structure of the EU we've got.

## 131

*'The battle of Britain is about to begin.*
*Upon this battle depends the survival of Christian civilisation.*
*Upon it depends our own British life, and the long continuity*
*of our institutions and our Empire. The whole fury and might*
*of the enemy must very soon be turned upon us...*
*Let us therefore brace ourselves to our duties,*
*and so bear ourselves that, if the British Empire and its*
*Commonwealth last for a thousand years,*
*men will still say: "This was their finest hour."*
WINSTON CHURCHILL, 1940

## 132

All of the major German political parties are (as is the case in the England) enthusiastic supporters of the European Union.

But I wonder how many people outside Germany realise just how big a part Germany plays in running the EU.

The new enlarged European Parliament has 732 members – compared to the old European Parliament which had 626 members. Before the EU was enlarged the Germans had 99 seats in the European Parliament. They still have 99 seats today.

Before the EU was enlarged the United Kingdom had 87 seats in the European Parliament. Today the United Kingdom has just 78 seats.

(We are told that the reduction in the UK's allocation of seats had to be made to allow for the new, incoming countries.)

Germany had 16% of the old EU Parliament.

Today Germany has 14% of the new EU Parliament.

England had 14% of the old EU Parliament.

Today the UK has under 11% of the new EU Parliament.

It doesn't seem entirely unfair to say that our influence in the EU is shrinking rather rapidly – certainly more rapidly than that of Germany, which has, let me remind you, 99 seats in the EU Parliament compared to England's 78.

I wonder how many Britons know this.

Did you?

Or did they forget to tell you?

## 133

If the EU fails, Germany will be left holding the EU's international reserves –all the gold handed over by the other countries.

One of the first things Labour did when coming into power was to give vast amounts of English gold to the EU. (We got euros in return.)

How generous of Blair and Brown to give away our money. And how very, very stupid.

## 134

*'The German is an expert on secret paths to chaos.'*
Nietzsche

## 135

One in five Germans believe that the USA engineered the attacks on America which took place on 11th September 2001 in order to create an excuse for more meddling in other countries. How will the EU's new Foreign Minister combine that view with England's so-called special relationship with the USA?

## 136

For decades now the two fundamental pillars of English foreign policy have been the so-called 'special relationship' with the USA (we do what they want us to do and use what is left of our fading reputation to give their aggressive, imperialistic ambitions some credibility and, in return, they ignore us when we want anything) and our membership of the developing European Union.

The Americans have never hidden the fact that they see England's enthusiasm for what our politicians call the 'special relationship' as a rather pathetic allegiance. In a fit of honesty, the American Secretary of State Dean Rusk once told Harold Wilson that 'the USA did not want to be the only country ready to intervene in any trouble spot in the world'. The Americans realised, many decades ago, that their plan to rule the world would arouse far less resentment among other nations if they were seen to have a sabre-waving ally. And in the most dangerous of their military adventures, of course, the Americans have used English troops as fodder for the enemy's guns.

Our 'special relationship' with the USA dates back to the 1940s when we were desperately trying to persuade the Americans to join in the Second World War.

(During the Second World War the USA made no secret of the fact that it saw the conflict as an opportunity to take over the role as global superpower and to displace England from those parts of the world which had for some years been coloured pink on the old-fashioned atlases. The Americans had already started to plan control of the entire non-Soviet world.)

There is today absolutely no evidence that English politicians have any influence over the USA.

Our link with the EU is rather more recent but dates back to the 1960s when civil servants decided that England had no future unless it became part of the burgeoning European State.

Back in 1968 the Foreign Office wrote that: 'If we want to exercise a major influence in shaping world events and are prepared to meet the costs we need to be influential with a much larger power system than we ourselves possess. The only practical possibilities open to us are to wield influence with Western Europe or the United States or both.'

But there is evidence that even the intellectually disadvantaged civil servants at the Foreign Office were aware of the dangers of attaching ourselves to American coat-tails.

A Foreign Office paper published in 1958 warned that 'the United Kingdom is already greatly dependent upon US support' but 'we must never allow this to develop to the point where we seem to be little more than an instrument of United States policy'.

Oh dear. Whoops.

It was civil service policy which misled Wilson into trying to take England into the EU and encouraged the treacherous Heath to succeed.

Back in the 1960s, Foreign Office civil servants regarded our membership of the Common Market as likely to enhance our 'special relationship' with the USA. And there is no doubt that it was to please America that England persisted in attempting to join the Common Market. In 1968 the Foreign Office warned that 'if we fail to become part of a more united Europe, England's links with the USA will not be enough to prevent us becoming increasingly peripheral to USA concerns.'

The Foreign Office believed that 'we can regain sufficient influence in world affairs to protect our interests overseas' by joining the EEC.

Bizarrely, and with an appalling lack of foresight and understanding, the Foreign Office stated that 'it is the hope of bringing our economic influence to bear more effectively in the political field that constitutes the principle motive of our application to join the EEC'.

Who were these anonymous Foreign Office civil servants who got it so completely wrong and betrayed their nation? How many of them had their grotesquely over-generous, index-linked pensions supplemented with knighthoods in reward for their stupidity and treachery? They should have all been shot as incompetent traitors.

Right from the start, America saw England as a Trojan Horse within the Common Market.

In 1966, American President Johnson was told by his Undersecretary of State that England should be 'applying her talents and resources to the leadership of Western Europe'. Johnson was advised that the USA should be encouraging England's membership of the EEC because this would suit American interests by providing the balance in Europe that 'might tend to check the dangerous tendencies which French nationalism is already producing.'

In other words, the Americans wanted us to join the EEC so that England could push the EEC into behaving in a way which the Americans wanted. We were also expected to keep America up-to-date with what the EEC was planning.

By 1972 the bright boys and girls at the Foreign Office had spotted this and were reporting that: 'The UK will, in its own interests, take on at times the role of Trojan Horse (in the EEC)...but its effectiveness in this role will depend on...not appearing to act as a US stooge.'

Even today, on the rare occasions when the Labour Party

opposes EU plans for the new federal state they do so not because they care about our disappearing culture and history but because some of the specific objectives (notably plans for EU military capability and decisions to sell weapons to China) are seen as contrary to American interests. The Americans, having created the EU, are now terrified that if the EU becomes a truly powerful force there is a considerable risk that Germany will pull the strings.

Those who argue that we should simply throw in our lot with the EU and help create a powerful federal Europe which can act as a counter-weight to the power of the USA are exhibiting great naivety and ignoring the fact that England joined the EU to please America and that our policy markers regard our major role within the EU as playing a supportive role to the USA.

Pathetically, civil servants in Whitehall, and English politicians, still regard the so-called 'special relationship' with the USA as our most important source of global power. We have, I'm afraid, become the equivalent of the under-developed teenager who hangs around with the class bully. When we mix with other gangs we do so because we are told to do it.

So we're caught between two stools. We get the worst of everything.

We are hated by Muslims everywhere for our support of America. We have become a major target for terrorists. We spend vast amounts of money supporting American brutality and carpet-bagging. To please the class bully our Government has accepted that English citizens can be extradited to America for trial there if that is what the Americans want. (Naturally, the process does not work both ways. English courts cannot demand that Americans be extradited to the UK.)

And we are surrendering our sovereignty to the EU, and handing over billions of pounds a year for the 'privilege' because that is what the Americans want. Our industry is being wrecked by red tape, regulations and legislation imported from both Washington and Brussels. Our nation is becoming steadily poorer.

The time has come for us to say thank you and goodbye to both the USA and the EU.

England can, and should, stand proud and alone.

It is the only dignified solution. It is the only way to regain our national self-respect.

## 137

Readers who have read both my books *England Our England* and *Rogue Nation* sometimes write to me to claim that it is crucial that we help the EU become a powerful superstate as a counterbalance and opposition to the United States of America.

What they perhaps do not realise is that the EU is very much a creation of the USA. The USA has been secretly funding and encouraging the growth of the EU since its very inception.

The Americans (with that peculiar brand of naivety which is going to cause them so much trouble) have always believed that a united Europe will be easier to deal with and easier to control. They even believe (and I know this is difficult to accept but please bear with me because it is true) that England will be able to persuade the rest of Europe to agree to join England in being a sort of American colony (and voting for America at the United Nations).

Sad, in a way, isn't it?

## 138

Gordon Brown claims that England needs to match America and 'unite around the next round of enterprise reforms and the drive towards a more dynamic entrepreneurial culture'.

(Who on earth writes the man's speeches and articles?)

'During the Industrial Revolution,' says Brown,' 'Britain

led the world in innovation, science and enterprise. It is time to rediscover that spirit and genius in the world of the Internet and digitalisation.'

Can Brown really be so out of touch that he doesn't know that his Government has (with the aid of the EU) more or less destroyed entrepreneurial activity in England? Is Gordon Brown really as stupid and out of touch with reality as he seems to be? (Can anyone, even a politician, be that stupid and that out of touch?)

Can Brown really be so stupefyingly stupid that he doesn't understand that the miles of red tape which his Government has produced (and the kilometres of red tape which the EU has foisted upon us) have strangled many small companies – and are destroying thousands more?

Can Brown really be so complacent, so arrogant and so utterly divorced from the real world that he doesn't realise that his Government has, under the leadership of the EU, created a bureaucracy-heavy world in which knowledgeable and ambitious young people realise that the only sensible career path lies in employment in a Government or local authority department?

Can Brown be so blind and busy patting himself on the back that he doesn't listen to anything anyone else says?

On the very day that he was crying out for more new businesses in England, the Association of Taxation Technicians, giving evidence to a House of Lords committee reviewing the Finance Bill, pointed out that the tax rises made in this year's Budget (and authored by Gordon Brown himself) meant that small firms' owners would find themselves going around in circles.

The Chancellor's small business tax policies have been described by accountants as 'hideously complex'.

Thanks to the help they have received from the EU, Brown and Labour have destroyed the entrepreneurial spirit in England.

Gordon Brown will only help England recover its position as a home for entrepreneurial spirits if he resigns and leaves public life as quickly as possible. But what the hell else could he do for a living? I wouldn't trust him to cut my lawn. However, if he promises never again to interfere with any aspect of English business life I will put on my doctor's hat and happily send him a sick note to last until he claims his fat cat Government pension. Brown is one person I'd prefer to see on permanent sick leave.

## 139

The unelected, overpaid bureaucrats who run the EU (and, therefore, our lives) don't like people who are independent. People who are independent ask too many questions and have a tendency to be difficult. The bureaucrats don't like the self-employed either. People who work for themselves (rather than for a large business) are too difficult to control and to keep tabs on. Large corporations are usually keen to cooperate with the bureaucrats. They can (and do) negotiate profitable quid pro quos. People who are self-employed threaten the system, are often annoyingly independent and invariably have little interest in cooperating with the bureaucrats.

It is hardly surprising, therefore, that the EU and the Government are doing their best to get rid of small businesses and the people who run them.

Three out of five new businesses now fail within their first three years. Most of the people whose businesses fail blame the same factors: increasing interference and red tape. Most of the interference and the red tape comes from the EU.

I believe the Government and the EU are working hard to improve the level of failure. I suspect that their immediate aim is to see four out of every five small businesses fail and ultimately, if things go according to plan, to see five out of five new businesses fail.

## 140

The EU has established a European Corporate Governance Forum to coordinate the corporate governance regimes of member states and to create new regulations. And the EU has already planned three new directives on company law, designed to stamp the EU's authority on corporate governance.

There will soon be yet more laws and yet more regulations controlling English companies. It will mean that legal, accounting and auditing costs will rocket, that bosses will have to spend more time dealing with paperwork and less time running their businesses, that companies which are on the edge will fail and that thousands of people will lose their jobs.

Experts are agreed that one thing a mass of new corporate governance regulations, guidelines, laws and rules will not do is prevent another corporate scandal. Fraudsters who want to lie and cheat and steal will simply ignore the new rules in the same way that they ignored the old ones.

These new rules and regulations will, of course, affect and afflict companies in other EU countries.

But English companies will suffer more than other companies in Europe because many, being listed on the American stock exchange, are also susceptible to onerous American regulations.

## 141

Thanks to the EU, employers are now legally required to consult employees about all decisions which may affect employment prospects.

Initially, from April 2005, the new regulations apply only to companies or 'undertakings' employing 150 or more people. But by April 2008 the new legislation will apply to companies employing as few as 50 people.

The new law has been widely ignored. Perhaps because it

was introduced in the run-up to a general election. Maybe because the EU introduces so many new laws that journalists and businessmen become glassy eyed when a new instruction is sent over from Brussels.

But this new EU law will have a devastating effect on businesses.

If the people running a company want to do something which might have an effect on employment prospects they now have to ask the employees for their approval.

It is, of course, difficult to think of anything a company might do which would not affect employment prospects.

If employees complain that they have not been properly consulted the company can be fined up to £75,000 for each offence.

## 142

Like businesses throughout the EU region, English businesses are being buried under new legislation. Since the EU-compliant Labour Party took over there have been 66 tax rises in England. Even more significantly, however, has been the increase in the number of new regulations. Labour claims to be 'friendly' towards business. This is another Labour lie. Every single day since Labour came to power they have introduced an average of 15 new regulations. It is clearly impossible for anyone running a small company to remain aware of what is, and is not, the law. And yet the penalties for ignoring these new rules are often serious.

EU rules and regulations (the miles of red tape produced by bureaucrats in Brussels) have resulted in massive unemployment in Europe. In many other European countries (including the large ones – France and Germany) the official level of unemployment is now running at between 10% and 15%. In England the figure has been kept lower than this (and has dropped to under a million), but only because the Labour Party has proved more adept at managing the figures than have other European governments. Only people who are receiving the 'jobseeker's' allowance are included in England's official figures. There are, in fact, another eight million people of working age who are not working and who are not looking for employment and who are (to use the official phrase) 'economically inactive'. The Government encourages this and there are financial incentives for the long-term unemployed to claim incapacity benefit rather than unemployment benefit. (Those who claim to be too stressed to work can receive around £90 a week, whereas those looking for work receive less than two thirds of this sum.)

## 143

Blair's Government has successfully kept unemployment figures low in five main ways.

First, although they pledged to cut welfare spending before they were first elected back in 1997 (Tony Blair made cutting the welfare burden a central part of his pre-election strategy telling voters: 'Judge me upon it – the buck stops with me') Labour has deliberately encouraged widespread fraud and has dramatically increased the number of people receiving incapacity or sickness benefit. Many of the 2.7 million allegedly 'on the sick' are suffering from common and often trivial health problems which don't necessarily stop more honest people from working. The vast majority of this 2.7 million have been too ill to work for over a year. Minor aches and pains (particularly backache) used to be favourite excuses but today the most popular complaints for those claiming incapacity benefit are ill-defined, difficult-to-prove mental disorders such as 'stress', 'anxiety' and 'depression'. Those claiming sick pay receive considerably more than those who are officially looking for jobs. I know that sounds too bizarre to be true but it is true. Unemployment costs the nation around £4 billion a year. Alleged incapacity costs the nation in excess of £16 billion a year.

Officially, doctors believe that a quarter of sick note requests are dubious and a fifth are just plain bogus. Unofficially, they believe that the figures should be reversed – with no more than a fifth of claims being honest. Once someone starts receiving sick pay they have a one in five chance of returning to work within five years. Once they have been off work for a year the average duration of their sick pay will be eight years. (For many the years of sick pay will merge neatly into years of pension.) Every year taxpayers hand over £2.4 billion in incapacity benefit to people who have nothing physically wrong with them but who claim that they are too 'stressed' to work. There are, according to the Government's own figures, now over a million people in England who receive long-term incapacity benefit for stress and similar conditions. One claimant, receiving a total of £37,400 a year in state handouts, said that he had been too depressed to work for seven years after the death of his father. In 2004 a Bank of England study estimated that 500,000 men had deliberately left their jobs to claim incapacity benefit because it was so generous. Many admitted that if they worked and paid tax they would take home less money than if they simply claimed benefits.

Even Labour Ministers themselves have had to admit that many of those claiming incapacity benefit are fit enough to work. According to a spokesperson for the Labour Government, a third of 2.7 million claimants could start work immediately and another third could return to work in 'the longer term'.

The spokesperson admitted that the Government had, for years, done 'almost nothing' to encourage people to come off incapacity benefit and confessed that only 3% of those living on incapacity benefit were actively trying to get employment. The Government won't do anything about this massive fraud (in which it is complicit) because if it did then the unemployment figures would rocket. And politically that just isn't acceptable.

The Government's second method of keeping the unemployment figures artificially low has been to increase the number of people on its own payroll. Since Labour took over the ruining of the country in 1997, Gordon Brown (who thinks he is a great Chancellor, has been a lucky Chancellor and whom history will show is probably one of the worst the country has ever had) has been hiring new Government employees at an average rate of 560 a day. The result is that in a period when English manufacturing industry lost a million jobs the Government's payroll increased by almost exactly the same number. A million productive workers have been replaced by a million parasitical bureaucrats who have a negative effect on the nation's productivity. (As a measure of the destruction of the English manufacturing industry it is worth noting that all the engineering companies quoted on the London stock exchange are worth less than a third of the value of just one German engineering business – Siemens. English industry has been destroyed by the EU because, unlike other governments in Europe, the English Government has insisted that its corporate citizens follow every new piece of legislation to the letter.)

And the Government is a generous payer. In 2005 the average hourly wage for Government employees was £11.32. That's £1.50 an hour more than the average wage in the private sector. And remember that Government employees work short hours, have excellent sick pay cover, suffer far less stress than employees in industry and can look forward to excellent index-linked pensions. It is hardly surprising that Government jobs are so popular. The English economy may seem to be doing well but it has been artificially sustained by Government spending, itself sustained by Government borrowing. For Gordon Brown to describe himself as a prudent Chancellor is as honest as it would be for Tony Blair to describe himself as a peace-loving Prime Minister.

It is hardly surprising that the rate of unemployment has

remained artificially low. One in five employed people in England now work for the Government. The vast majority of the new jobs have been for bureaucrats doing worthless and entirely unnecessary jobs. Indeed, most of the jobs are worse than useless in that they involve creating new paperwork and enforcing pointless new EU regulations which slow down the work of those who are trying to do real jobs. Government ministers repeatedly promise to cull civil service jobs but instead of cutting the number of public service employees the Government has consistently increased the taxpayers' burden.

(The added advantage, to the Government, of all these Government employees is, of course, that many will vote Labour in order to keep their jobs. The Government is using taxpayers' money to ensure that it remains in power.)

The third way the Government artificially keeps the unemployment figures low is by providing a variety of schemes allegedly designed to 'train' and 'prepare' the unemployed for work. Everyone involved (employees and 'employees') knows that these schemes are fraudulent and that their sole purpose is to help the Government massage the official figures.

The most cynical scheme of all is, perhaps, the policy of encouraging teenagers to carry on with full-time education for as long as possible. Since students now have to pay for their fees this scheme doesn't cost the Government a great deal but it does keep vast numbers of young people off the unemployment register. The colleges and universities which have been set up to provide education for this vast army of students have been encouraged to offer courses which are not intellectually demanding and which offer attractive-sounding subjects for study. It is cheaper to teach cake decorating and nail filing than it is to teach dentistry or plumbing. And cake decorating and nail filing are doubtless easier to learn too. So, as a result, a nation which is desperately short of dentists and plumbers, is now awash with hairdressers, brewers and nail technicians while countless others are graduating with utterly worthless or impractical diplomas in media studies, film-making and tourism.

Finally, the Government has one other way of 'reducing' the unemployment figures. It is called the 'head-in-the-sand' technique. There are more than one million people in England who are under the age of 25 and who are neither working nor studying. None of these people (and there are, remember, a million of them) count towards the official unemployment figures because they are not actively seeking work.

## 144

As England adopts more EU regulations so her attractiveness to employers falls. During the 1980s and 1990s England was a popular and competitive location for big companies who wanted a toe in Europe but who didn't want to be suffocated by the EU's red tape.

Today, as Labour brings more and more EU legislation into the country, foreign investment is falling dramatically. For example, foreign investment in England fell from £15.6 billion in 2002 to £8.1 billion in 2003. Professional advisers are now telling multinational companies not to come to England.

Labour's high tax policies haven't helped, of course, but it is the EU regulations which are scaring away multinationals and threatening England's future financial stability.

To regain our national strength we need to leave the EU and get rid of all the daft laws and regulations with which we have been saddled.

(And we need to get rid of Labour – which is committed to wasting vast amounts of taxpayers' money. As fewer and fewer companies open factories and offices in England, and the ones which are here decide to leave, so the tax burden on the companies remaining will grow. And as hard working citizens give up and emigrate so taxes on individuals will have to soar.)

## 145

There are now so many EU laws that it is virtually impossible for anyone to get through a day without breaking several. When there are so many laws that no one knows what they are, and everyone regularly breaks them without thought, knowledge or regret, then respect for the law disappears. But it is not just respect for the small laws which disappears: respect for the big laws goes too. The EU has devalued the law and our attitude towards it.

## 146

The EU bureaucrats are demanding an 'evaluation of the quality of justice' in the EU. They want a 'European judicial culture'.

And they are getting it.

In order to allay our fears the bureaucrats say that they will 'respect legal traditions' in individual countries.

But their idea of 'respect' is clearly not the same as mine.

The EU has already failed to respect English legal traditions with the introduction of its pan-European 'arrest warrant' whereby suspects can be arrested without the need for anything as inconvenient as 'evidence'.

The EU bureaucrats (perhaps we should call them 'masters' because that is a better description of their role in our lives) want 'common standards of procedure in criminal proceedings'. The EU will in future be responsible for defining both criminal offences and penalties. The aim is to 'increase the efficiency of prosecutions' and to secure more convictions.

It is undoubtedly for this reason that Blair's Labour Government, with Home Secretaries Straw and Blunkett, has been busy attempting to get rid of such inconvenient legal nonsenses as trial by jury. It is far easier to get convictions when the decision about whether or not a defendant should be found guilty can be left in the hands of a judiciary led by the Prime Minister's friends and former flat mates.

## 147

'The people must not take the law into their own hands,' said an EU bureaucrat.

Whose law is it, then?

## 148

The EU is introducing what it calls 'intelligence-led law enforcement' throughout Europe. There will be 'new centralised European databases' and 'no gaps in surveillance' by security services.

The new 'intelligence-led law enforcement' will be designed to enable the EU to stop 'peaceful but noisy protests' and to put an end to 'lobbying to change government policy'.

Read that paragraph again. Aloud.

## 149

The fundamental difference between English justice and French justice is that we were given our basic rights (in the Magna Carta) whereas the French took theirs (as a result of the French Revolution). The EU is now imposing the French legal traditions on England. The result is that we are acquiring a legal system which we don't understand and don't know how to use and don't feel comfortable with.

## 150

The European Court of Justice (ECJ), which follows the concept of corpus juris (an idea which is quite alien to English Common Law) has now successfully supplanted the traditional English legal system. The ECJ in Strasbourg is a higher court than anything in England. It exists, at least in part, to ensure the integration of separate EU countries into the new state of Europe. It can and does make new, irrevocable laws to govern the citizens of the individual countries which are now part of the new Europe.

The independence and freedom of English citizens, and of England itself, were built upon English Common Law (one of England's greatest gifts to the world). It was English Common Law, with the principles of trial by jury and *habeas corpus*, which guaranteed our liberty.

No more.

The European Commission, run by unelected bureaucrats, has pushed aside centuries of English law and replaced it with European law. The European Court of Justice exists not to guarantee the freedom and liberty of individual citizens but to protect the corrupt and dishonest bureaucrats who now rule our lives.

(It is worth remembering that although the English Government has always obeyed the European Court of Justice, other governments are not so obedient. After English beef exports had been banned as a result of the Mad Cow crisis the ECJ eventually ruled that imports could be allowed again. The French Government merrily ignored the ECJ ruling and continued to refuse to accept English beef. Naturally, the French were allowed to get away with this.)

## 151

The major mainland European economies are in a mess and are trapped in a vicious circle. Politicians and bureaucrats don't have the intelligence or the will to produce a solution.

Low growth has led to high unemployment which has to a certain extent been disguised by a massive rise in the number of people employed by governments or receiving sick pay.

All across Europe huge numbers of potential workers are drawing welfare benefits; as single mothers, because they have retired early or because they are classified as too ill to work.

Around 40% of Europeans of working age are economically inactive, acting as a drain on their economies, rather than contributing in any way. (The size of this problem in EU can be judged from the fact that in America the comparative figure is 29%.)

I have described the size of the problem in England earlier in this book. But the problem is by no means exclusively an English one. In the Netherlands, for example, around 1 million of a working population of nine million are classified as disabled. As in England most of them are suffering from stress-related disorders.

The inevitable result of this has been higher social expenditure, leading to higher taxes, leading to reduced earnings, leading to lower growth, leading to lower earnings, leading to lower tax revenue, leading to higher taxes, leading to...well, you get the picture and see what I meant about a vicious circle.

While unregulated low-cost countries such as China and India boom, highly regulated high-cost countries in the EU are in terminal decline.

The only way out of the downward spiral is for countries of the EU to cut the expenditure by their various governments and to cut red tape.

The age at which individuals receive government financed pensions will have to rise and the number of people on welfare will have to fall. If this is not done the welfare systems across Europe will collapse and benefits will have to be withdrawn. There will, inevitably, be protests (probably violent) from people who have spent decades (often their whole lives) living on benefits and who know of no other way of life.

So far, all attempts to extend the working lives of those who work and to cut back the payments to those who don't have been disastrous. Governments in Germany, France and Italy have tried to do something about this but have found themselves widely attacked. Feeble attempts to deal with the problem in England have been squashed by the unions.

It is now considered politically unacceptable to do anything about a problem which is not only unavoidable but which is getting worse and worse each day.

Despite the appalling economic management by Labour, England is still in a better condition than most other countries in the EU. There are two reasons for this.

First, England is still not in the euro and is, therefore, to a certain extent protected from the damage.

Second, although the Government hasn't saved anything to pay for pensions, individuals have. Pensions in England are in a mess but individual Englishmen and women have saved billions for their retirement. Although much of that money has been stolen, squandered or lost there is still quite a bit of it left.

If England eventually votes 'yes' to the new constitution we will have to join the euro. Our savings will then disappear into a central EU pension fund and we will have to suffer because of the wastefulness and stupidity of the French and the Germans.

The only way for England to save itself is to leave the EU.

# 152

The fates of all EU nations are tied together both politically and economically. All 25 members of the EU are shackled to one another by an impenetrable and destructive network of economic and social policies. As economic problems mount the political tensions will get worse. Meanwhile, the EU's answer is to create more red tape, to introduce more social legislation giving workers more and more rights, to introduce more onerous environmental legislation, to offer more state subsidies, to encourage additional payments to those who say that they cannot work. The unelected bureaucrats in Brussels are actively making the problems worse. If they wanted to create chaos they could not do a better job of it. (A fact which rather supports the fears of those who believe in some sort of global conspiracy.)

## 153

The basic building blocks for a growing economy are incentives and personal interest and a controlled bureaucracy (because bureaucracy suffocates enterprise). The EU removes incentives and personal interest and stifles entrepreneurs with bureaucracy. Is it any wonder that European economies are stagnating?

## 154

*'Some committed Europhiles frankly acknowledge that, at times, they have deliberately disguised quite profound changes as mere technical adjustments to avoid causing popular alarm. Jean-Claude Juncker, the Prime Minister of Luxembourg and the EU's longest-serving head of government, explains: 'We decide on something, leave it lying around and wait and see what happens. If no one kicks up a fuss, because most people don't know what has been decided, we continue step by step until there is no turning back.'*
THE ECONOMIST 25.9.04
(ALWAYS A STAUNCH SUPPORTER OF THE EU)

## 155

France, Germany and Italy were, before the introduction of the euro, among the world's most prosperous and technologically advanced countries. These nations are now sinking fast. Their industries (and jobs) are under siege. The euro has destroyed living standards, is destroying culture and, by destroying economic strength, is destroying the influence of those countries which signed up for it.

# 156

EU laws mean that any small employer who employs a woman of child-bearing age (or, indeed employs any man with a wife or partner of child-bearing age) must be stark raving bonkers.

Thanks to EU legislation, employers have to allow female members of staff to take up to nine months off if they have a baby. And new fathers can have time off too.

The new parents will, of course, receive money as a reward for their fecundity. Some of the money will come from their proud employer and some from long-suffering taxpayers and it will be paid for the whole of their post-natal rest period. The employer has to keep the job open while the new parent is learning to change nappies and burp the baby.

And it is the disruption this causes, rather than just the financial cost, which is so destructive to small businesses.

The EU bureaucrats who thought up this nonsense work in an environment where money is no object and where any employee can disappear for years at a time without anyone noticing.

But, for example, a small businessman who employed a husband and wife team to run his shop would be ruined by such legislation.

No wonder more and more small employers now prefer to hire older staff.

I can't help wondering how long it will be before the EU insists that conception leave should be made available for couples who want to start a family.

# 157

As I have constantly predicted since its inception and introduction the euro is a disaster.

The original plan – indeed, the assumption, was that all national members of the EU would abandon their national currencies and adopt the euro.

But first Denmark and then Sweden voted to reject membership of the single currency. Both proved that it was possible to survive happily without the euro.

In the summer of 2005, dissatisfaction with the euro reached a high and it began to look as though the euro had only a very limited life expectancy. If the euro had relatives they would, in June 2005, have already been gathered by the bedside awaiting the worst. The collapse of the euro, incidentally, had nothing whatsoever to do with the rejection of the EU constitution.

In France, the enthusiasm for the euro has always been so slight that prices in the shops have been shown in euros and old-fashioned francs (with the price in francs still often being given priority even in 2005).

By the time that France and Holland rejected the EU constitution it was clear that the days of the euro were numbered. In June 2005, Italy's welfare minister called for his country to hold a referendum on whether or not Italy should abandon the euro and bring back the lira. The Italians were blaming the euro for rocketing prices. Italian experts claimed that their country's economy had been crippled because the interest rates set by the European Central Bank were too high for their country.

In France and Germany (where unemployment levels have been between 10% and 15% since the introduction of the new currency) the euro is widely blamed for the economic problems the two countries are struggling to deal with. The Dutch claim that the value of the euro makes them feel poor.

Early in the summer of 2005, the Germans were talking about quitting the euro and going back to their beloved mark. Germany officials were secretly discussing the possibility that the euro might collapse. Leading French politicians talked about changing the rules which govern economies within the eurozone and dumping the so-called stability pact set up to force countries to abide by strict rules on allowable budget deficits.

There is little doubt that if referendums on the euro were held throughout Europe the result would be an overwhelming vote of no confidence in the single currency.

Throughout all this the English Labour Government has maintained its enthusiasm for the euro and its determination to abandon the pound sterling and take England into the euro as and when they think the time is right (for which read, when they think they can trick the public into accepting the decision).

Can there have ever been a more bizarre example of rats actually wanting to board a sinking ship?

# 158

France and Germany both ignore the EU's rules when it suits them.

All members of the EU are linked together and nations which share a common currency (the euro) are tied to one another particularly tightly.

Normally, when an individual country runs into financial trouble, its government can put up interest rates or devalue its currency. But in Europe this isn't possible. Right at the beginning, before the euro was introduced, even the intellectually disadvantaged bureaucrats of the EU realised that this could cause problems and that the citizens of individual countries which were careful and responsible might end up supporting the citizens of countries with less responsible governments.

To try to prevent this happening the EU drew up a 'stability and growth pact' requiring all countries sharing the euro to keep their budget deficits below 3% of GDP at all times.

When Portugal exceeded the 3% deficit, the Portuguese Government tried to do the right thing: they slashed public spending. This pushed up unemployment and made the local recession worse. The Portuguese paid heavily for their profligacy.

But France and Germany don't consider that they play by the same rules. When both France and Germany broke the 3% rule they simply ignored the pact and told other countries that the rule didn't apply to them. The European Court of Justice insisted that France and Germany had to obey the rules like everyone else. France and Germany just ignored the Court. EU ministers in Brussels eventually agreed to drop any disciplinary action against them. 'These rules were not invented for us,' said the French and German Governments.

France and Germany have now violated the 3% limit on budget deficits for three years in a row and a whole filing cabinet full of exceptions have been devised and published to ensure that they can now easily evade sanctions in a way that would make veteran tax evaders grin with delight.

Any future economic security the EU might have hoped for has now been banished. The EU is doomed.

Ironically, in the summer of 2005, France and Germany were two of the first countries to talk publicly about the possibility of abandoning the euro and reverting, respectively, to the franc and the deutschmark.

## 159

Greece breached the euro area's budget deficit ceiling of 3% of GDP every year between 1998 and 2003. The Greeks even breached the rules in the years when they supposedly met the Masstricht criteria for entering the euro. The Greeks went unpunished for their sins.

An English greengrocer who sold bananas by the pound was arrested and imprisoned.

## 160

As several countries (including France, Germany and Italy) discuss the possibility of abandoning the euro and reverting to their own traditional currencies it is worth remembering that just a few years ago those of us who opposed the euro were regarded as financial Luddites.

## 161

Just about every despot and tyrant in history has used 'national security' as an excuse for passing laws which restrict the freedom of individuals. England's Labour Government, working in conjunction with the EU, now regularly uses the alleged terrorist threat as an excuse for taking away our freedom. Rarely have so many liars told so many lies to so many people.

## 162

The EU has, virtually since its inception, been a playground for criminals – some of them working for the organisation and some of them simply taking advantage of the stupidity, incompetence or dishonesty of those working for it. In the days when the EU was still known as the EEC a number of entrepreneurs got rich by taking advantage of the EEC's confusion of import-export subsidies and the EEC's Common Agricultural Policy which provides farmers and traders throughout Europe with protected prices and subsidies which guarantee them profits. It is these subsidies and guarantees which have led to the creation of the EEC's most famous creations: butter mountains and wine lakes.

The first rogues to take advantage of this scheme bought a trainload of butter which they then sent on a Grand European Tour, visiting only countries which were members of the EEC. Every time the train passed over a frontier the tricksters would claim a massive subsidy from the EEC, simply filling in a few forms to confirm that they intended to convert the butter into another product. At the end of the train's Grand Tour, after pocketing millions of deutschmarks in subsidies, they would stop the train and sell the butter for what they had paid for it.

Once this scheme became known other adventurers decided to take advantage of it and soon the railways and roads of Europe were congested with trains and lorries packed with travelling produce. The cost to European taxpayers was phenomenal. Before long the tricksters realised that actually buying the damned butter and paying for it to be carried around Europe was an unnecessary expense. All they had to do was *claim* that they had bought the butter (or whatever). The transactions existed only on paper.

When it became clear that it was possible to fool the EEC simply by filling in forms a whole new generation of fraudsters decided to join in. Another popular scheme involved claiming value added tax rebates on goods which were alleged to be travelling between one EEC country and another.

The bureaucrats in Brussels, who were either embarrassed by all this or angry because they weren't being given big enough pay-offs themselves, constantly changed the regulations in order to try to stop these activities. But their attempts were futile. Every time they sealed up one loophole another one appeared.

The fraudsters who helped themselves to millions in this way were, of course, never prosecuted. Even when they were identified there was no effective means of starting a prosecution. In which country had the fraud taken place? In what country had the criminal law been broken? Where should the prosecution be initiated? The problem was that no criminal law had been broken. The EEC wasn't a country. There was no one able to prosecute. And so the fraudsters went free and tottered off to Switzerland with their millions. (Of course, it is doubtful if the EEC would have wanted to prosecute even if they had been able. Prosecuting would have merely drawn attention to the problem and made the EEC look even more foolish and pointless in the public's eyes.)

## 163

The Members of the European Parliament get perks worth £140 million a year. That works out at a little over £175,000 a year per MEP.

Naturally, MEPs also receive a substantial salary.

## 164

The EU is a rest home for political debris; floating contentedly in a stagnant sea of greed, self-interest and corruption. The EU and the Labour Party go together well and no one illustrates the link better than the Kinnocks.

Kinnock was a European Commissioner and his wife an MEP and according to one estimate the pair of them were raking in £500,000 a year from various wages and benefits paid out by the EU.

Kinnock was European Commissioner in charge of anti-corruption in the EU. (No giggling. This is serious.) Sadly, he wasn't enormously successful in dealing with the problem. Indeed, the National Audit Office reported that the amount of 'waste' had doubled in the year after he took over and 10,000 individual cases of corruption were uncovered. (Naturally, no one knows how many remained uncovered.)

When a brave woman who worked for the European Commission turned whistleblower and spoke out she, like a long line of other whistleblowers, discovered that telling the truth about EC crookedness is not a wise career move.

She was subjected to threats and harassment.

Kinnock was not sacked and did not resign although he had initially dismissed her valid claims.

(No EU officials were punished although £3 million of EU funds had disappeared. All the accused are either still working for the EU or have retired on full pensions. But the journalist who broke the story was arrested by the Belgian police on false charges, made up by the European Commission.)

Now that he has retired from the EU, Kinnock will get a pension of £63,900 a year from a pension pot worth more than £2 million. (Curiously, that is £500,000 more than Englishmen and women who save towards their own pensions will be allowed to accumulate under new Government legislation).

Kinnock, who once described the House of Lords as nothing more than descendants of brigands, muggers, bribers and gangsters, has now entered the House of Lords.

I hope he feels at home there, surrounded, as he will be, by so many of Tony's other cronies.

## 165

*'For the past eight years the Court (the European Court of Auditors)*
*has had to refuse to issue the required 'Statement of Assurance'*
*that money has been properly spent.'*
THE TIMES, 17.3.2004

## 166

There was widespread laughter around Europe, particularly among those who know how the EU works, when the EU was said to have reservations about Bulgaria becoming a member of the EU because of internal corruption. The words pot, kettle and black were widely translated.

## 167

One EU official was found to have created false travel documents and to have claimed £465,000 for meetings which were never held.

## 168

*'The only real and consistent beneficiaries of the EU's Common Agricultural Policy are the fraudsters and organised crime.'*
FROM *THE OCTOPUS* BY BRIAN FREEMANTLE, 1995

## 169

Almost half of the EU's annual budget of £75 billion is spent on the Common Agricultural Policy – and handed out as subsidies to farmers.

The EU's Common Agricultural Policy puts up the price of our food, destroys English farmers and impoverishes the poor in developing countries. The Common Agricultural Policy is one of the main reasons for the epidemic of starvation in Africa.

The Common Agricultural Policy (the stone around the EU's neck) was designed to keep the prices of food artificially high and to provide subsidies and high tariffs for small French and German farmers.

## 170

Our 30-year membership of the EU has cost England an estimated £75 billion in membership fees.

## 171

*'The official Court of Auditors agreed figure for theft, each year, from the Common Agricultural Policy, is £2.5 billion. No one in the Commission – or, unofficially, in the Court of Auditors – disputes the more accurate figure to be £6 billion: I have even heard it put as high as £10 billion.'*
FROM *THE OCTOPUS* BY BRIAN FREEMANTLE, 1995

## 172

When you hear people talk about democracy in Europe, remember that the European Parliament exists only to rubber stamp new laws made up by the unelected European Commission and its bureaucrats. Members of the EU Parliament cannot veto the work of the European Commission.

## 173

Back in 1967, work was started on a new building for the EU. The European Commission immediately leased the building from the Belgium Government. After EU staff moved into the building in 1991 it was discovered that the whole erection was stuffed with asbestos. The staff evacuated themselves. (They must have done. I can't imagine that anyone else cared enough to tell them to get out.)

In 1995, the bureaucrats finally got round to organising the removal of the asbestos from the now empty building. This took another four years.

Naturally, we paid for the whole of this disaster.

We spent £370 million buying the offices in the centre of Brussels. And we forked out another £338 million of our money to renovate the building. And we paid out £96 million in rent so that the bureaucrats would have somewhere else to put their filing cabinets while the improvements took place.

Much of the cost of repairing and renovating this wretched building has been the result of bureaucrats behaving like bureaucrats. For example, they spent 12 weeks trying to decide on the type of light bulbs to put in the building.

The man responsible for at least some of this wonderful work was a certain Mr Neil Kinnock.

## 174

The construction of both the Scottish Parliament building and the European Parliament building went way over budget. Hundreds of millions of pounds were wasted.

Economist Milton Friedman was right when he observed that the best purchases are made by people spending their own money.

## 175

The EU has two main HQs, one in Brussels in Belgium and one in Strasbourg in France. Once a month a convoy of lorries moves documents from Brussels to Strasbourg (and then back again). This entirely pointless exercise costs £70 million a year.

## 176

In contrast to other European countries, English citizens have the right to *habeas corpus*. The principle of *habeas corpus* was already common law by the time the Magna Carta was signed in 1215. The principle was enshrined in law when the *Habeas Corpus* Act was passed in 1679. The Latin phrase translates as: 'you should have the body' and it means that under this Act a judge can order the Government to bring anybody in its custody to a specified court for a trial to ensure that he is tried according to the due process of law. The purpose of the Act was to stop the Government imprisoning people without good reason. We are about to lose this right and for this we can thank the EU.

## 177

*'To no man will we sell, or deny, or delay, right or Justice.'*
CLAUSE 40, THE MAGNA CARTA

# 178

*'No free man shall be taken or imprisoned or dispossessed, or outlawed or exiled, or in any way destroyed, not will we go upon him, nor will we send against him except by the lawful judgement of his peers or by the law of the land.'*
CLAUSE 39, *THE MAGNA CARTA*

# 179

The new legal system which the EU (and Labour) is imposing on England will mean the end of the Magna Carta. There will be no juries, the authorities will be able to lock you up without trial and if, when you do come to trial you are found not guilty, the state will be able to keep re-trying you until they get the 'right' verdict.

# 180

When it was introduced in the year 2000, Blair's Government claimed that The Human Rights Act was merely a 'tidying up exercise'. (Those are the three words which Government ministers invariably use to describe every storm of bureaucratic nonsense from Brussels. They used the same words to describe the new EU constitution.) What the Government didn't bother to tell us was that the Human Rights Act is a 100% creation of European bureaucrats and changes our world completely.

The Human Rights Act has been used by terrorists, criminals, and illegal asylum seekers and a whole host of others. It has been used by gypsies or travellers to enable them to breach planning laws. It is, so we are told, the Human Rights Act which is responsible for much of the politically correct nonsense which now besieges our society. It is the Human Rights Act which explains much of the blatant injustice in our society.

There is little doubt that there are few things which have damaged the very fabric of English society more than the Human Rights Act.

But everyone can use the Human Rights Act. That is the whole point of it.

Even the English can use it.

Here is a summary of the articles of the Human Rights Act. It shouldn't take you too long to see how you too can take advantage of this probably well-meaning but impractical legislation.

At the end of the list of 'Articles' I have added a list of protocols (later additions to the Convention). If you read through these carefully I feel sure that you may find ways to take advantage of some of these 'rights' too. (Ironically, I consider that much of the EU's own legislation is in breach of the Human Rights legislation.)

*Article 1: (is the introduction).*

*Article 2: Right to Life.*
You have the absolute right to have your life protected by law. There are only certain very limited circumstances where it is acceptable for the State to take away someone's life, e.g. if a police officer acts justifiably in self defence.

*Article 3: Prohibition of Torture.*
You have the absolute right not to be tortured or subjected to treatment or punishment which is inhuman or degrading.

*Article 4: Prohibition of Slavery and Forced Labour.*
You have the absolute right not to be treated as a slave or forced to perform certain kinds of labour.

*Article 5: Right To Liberty And Security*
You have the right not to be deprived of your liberty – 'arrested or detained' – except in limited cases specified in the Article (e.g. where you are suspected or convicted of committing a crime) and where this is justified by a clear legal procedure.

*Article 6: Right To A Fair Trial*

You have the right to a fair and public hearing within a reasonable period of time. This applies to both criminal charges against you, or in sorting out cases concerning your civil rights and obligations. Hearings must be by an independent and impartial tribunal established by law. It is possible to exclude the public from the hearing (though not the judgement) if that is necessary to protect things like national security or public order. If it is a criminal charge you are presumed innocent until proved guilty according to law and have certain guaranteed rights to defend yourself.

*Article 7: No Punishment Without Law*

You normally have the right not to be found guilty of an offence arising out of actions which at the time you committed them were not criminal. You are also protected against later increases in the possible sentence for an offence.

*Article 8: Right To Respect For Private And Family Life*

You have the right to respect for your private and family life, your home and your correspondence. This right can only be restricted in specified circumstances (such as protecting the public health or safety, preventing crime and protecting the rights of others.)

*Article 9: Freedom of Thought, Conscience and Religion*

You are free to hold a broad range of views, beliefs and thoughts, as well as religious faith. Limitations are permitted only in specified circumstances (such as protecting the public health or safety, preventing crime and protecting the rights of others).

*Article 10: Freedom of Expression*

You have the right to hold opinions and express your views on your own or in a group. This applies even if they are unpopular or disturbing. This right can only be restricted in specified circumstances (such as protecting the public health or safety, preventing crime and protecting the rights of others).

*Article 11: Freedom of Assembly and Association*
You have the right to assemble with other people in a peaceful way. You also have the right to associate with people, which can include the right to form a trade union. These rights can only be restricted in specified circumstances (such as protecting the public health or safety, preventing crime and protecting the rights of others).

*Article 12: Right To Marry*
Men and women have the right to marry and start a family. The national law will still govern how and what age this can take place.

*Article 13: There is no article 13.*

*Article 14: Prohibition of Discrimination*
In the application of the Convention rights, you have the right not to be treated differently because of your race, religion, sex, political views or any other status, unless this can be justified objectively. Everyone must have equal access to Convention rights, whatever their status.

*Article 1 of Protocol 1: Protection of Property*
You have the right to the peaceful enjoyment of your possessions. Public authorities cannot usually interfere with things you own or the way you use them except in specified limited circumstances.

*Article 2 of Protocol 1: Right To Education*
You have the right not to be denied access to the educational system.

*Article 3 of Protocol 1: Right To Free Elections*
Elections for members of the legislative body (e.g. Parliament) must be free and fair and take place by secret ballot. Some qualifications may be imposed on those that are eligible to vote (e.g. a minimum age).

## 181

The Human Rights Act must be obeyed by all public authorities (Government Ministers, civil servants, your local authority, your health authority and agencies such as the police, the courts and private companies when carrying out public functions). All new laws must fit in with your rights under the Human Rights Act.

One of the specific rights given by the Human Rights Act is the fundamental right to assembly – a right to meet with others for whatever reason you like (as long as it is lawful). If the police or public authorities are thinking of banning a demonstration, or restricting marches, they cannot impose a blanket ban. They cannot go further than is necessary to guard against the expected risks to others.

## 182

*'Prosperity is not a gift from the government or anyone else. Free enterprise, not government, is the source from which our blessings flow.'*
RONALD REAGAN

## 183

The EU had hoped (through the EU Food Supplements Directive) to ban many of the vitamins and minerals sold in England and considered essential for good health by many people. A total of 5,000 products would have been banned, though people would have still been able to buy products sold by the large, international drug companies. Indeed, the only people in favour of the legislation were, it seems, the large, international drug companies. In the end the European Court of Justice Advocate General claimed that the EU Food Supplements Directive was flawed.

# 184

'*By the year 2020 one third of the population in the developed world will be over the age of sixty-five. One quarter of the population will be diabetic. In every home where there are two healthy parents and two healthy children there will be four disabled or dependant individuals needing constant care. Diseases such as diabetes and schizophrenia (which are genetically transmitted) and blindness (which is ten times as common among the over sixty-fives and thirty times as common among the over seventy-fives) will be as common as indigestion and hay fever are today. Unemployment will be normal. Stress-related diseases will be endemic. Developed countries around the world will face bankruptcy as they struggle to find the cash to pay pensions, sick pay and unemployment benefits.*

*Resentment, bitterness and anger will divide the young and the old, the able bodied and the dependant, the employed and the unemployed. There will be anarchy, despair and civil war. There will be ghettoes of elderly and disabled citizens abandoned to care for themselves. There will be armed guards on our hospitals. Those with jobs will travel to work in armoured cars.*

*For years those who have forecast the end of the human race have talked of nuclear war, starvation in the third world and pollution as being the major threats to our survival. But the decline I predict for the year 2020 will be triggered not by any of these forces but by much simpler and entirely predictable developments. The human race will be destroyed by medical ambition, commercial greed and political opportunism.*

*In those last desperate years as our species destroys itself, attempts will be made to restore the balance. Euthanasia will be widely advocated. Politicians will call for parents to submit to genetic checks before being issued with breeding licences. Murder will be seen as a social service. But it will be too late. By the year 2020 there will be no chance for us to avoid the inevitable. The decline of our species will continue rapidly.*'

The paragraphs above were taken from the Prologue to my book *The Health Scandal* which I wrote in the mid-1980s and which was first published in 1988.

When the book was being prepared for publication the publishers (Sidgwick and Jackson) were wildly enthusiastic about its prospects and expressed themselves eager to promote the book as widely as possible. But suddenly, and without explanation, things changed. The book came out without even a whimper – let alone a bang. There was so little publicity that I sent out a press release myself – and was told off by the publishers for doing so. The book was remaindered very quickly and no real effort was made to sell the paperback rights. (When Sidgwick and Jackson insisted that the paperback rights could not be sold my agent took back the rights. She sold the paperback rights in days. This was curious because it meant that we did not have to share the financial proceeds from the paperback sale with Sidgwick & Jackson). Not for the only time in my life, I got the impression that a book of mine had been effectively suppressed by its own publisher. It was the way this book was treated which was one of the triggers for me to start publishing my own work.)

The fears I first expressed in the mid-1980s do not now seem quite so outrageous. Many of the predictions I made in that book are coming true. And rather than doing anything to help prevent the coming crisis the bureaucrats of the EU have made things worse. Their miles of red tape have created a sclerotic economy and their desperate attempts to lower the average age in western European countries by encouraging immigration is creating social unrest and a right wing political backlash. Every action of the EU seems to have been designed to ensure that my worst fears come true.

## 185

A survey conducted by Deutsche Bank reported that by 2050 there will be 75 pensioners for every 100 workers in the EU. (There will, of course, also be many people who are younger than this but who are, for a variety of reasons, unwilling or unable to work.)

These fundamental demographic changes are being produced by reduced infant mortality rates and, most importantly, by falling birth rates. Back in the 1960s there were many scare stories about the population time bomb and couples were encouraged not to have more than two children. More significantly, however, the cost of raising more than two children has become an intolerable burden for those who have to earn a living and pay taxes. Women are having children later and are leaving larger gaps between children. In modern England, and indeed in much of modern Europe, only those who live on State handouts are able to feed and care for more than two children. (The State is, therefore, ensuring that future generations will largely be brought up by the lazy, the feckless and the incapable.)

This dramatic ageing of the European population will have a significant impact on the potential for economic growth and on the demand from pensioners for financial support and for health care.

Since state pensions are paid out of current tax revenues (and are no better than illegal Ponzi schemes) either taxes or national debts will have to rise steeply. Standard and Poor's (a credit-rating agency) has predicted that France and Germany, the two EU countries with the most serious pension problems, could see their public debt grow to more than 200% of GDP by the year 2050. This would clearly be unsustainable. (It is hardly surprising that the other EU countries are loathe to see England leave the EU. Far more private pension money has been saved by the English than by any other nationality. The EU wants to share those savings and England's accumulated pension funds are likely to be raided by other European countries on the grounds that when the EU is a single State, savings will become community property.)

Our politicians don't seem to have grasped the awful significance of the changes that are coming. We will need fewer schools and more old people's homes but our politicians are busy building more schools and because of EU regulations we have fewer old people's homes than ever. Youthful spenders will be replaced by middle-aged savers desperately trying to accumulate a little money to help ease their way through old age and to help pay for medical and dental care. The number of workers struggling to pay the costs of all those receiving sickness benefits and all those receiving pensions will keep falling. The working classes who had become the middle classes will become the working classes again; they will work harder than ever, earn less than ever and pay more tax than ever. (State employees don't count as contributors since they too are a drag on the economy. Their salaries and pensions must be paid for by the efforts of a diminishing number of private sector workers.)

European politicians either didn't see what was coming or else they kept their eyes averted because they couldn't bear to look.

Now, however, it is no longer possible to ignore the impending crisis. (Actually, it's too late. It is now up to each and every man and woman to look after themselves. Anyone (other than an ex-MP or ex-civil servant) who relies on the Government to provide for them in their old age will spend their final years cold and hungry. If England manages to get out of the EU taxes are going to have to rise dramatically. If we stay in the EU taxes are going to have to rise far more than dramatically as English taxpayers struggle to help pay the pension deficits in France and Germany.)

Sudden (and belated awareness) of this looming disaster helps to explain much of what is now going on in Europe.

It is because of this problem that European governments are desperately (though unsuccessfully) trying to reform their pension schemes. And it is because of this impending crisis that legislation has been introduced giving older workers more protection. (The EU needs private sector employees to carry on working well into their seventies. The new legislation is designed to ensure that employers cannot discriminate against employees on the basis of age. State employees, public sector workers will, of course, still be entitled to retire as early as 50 and will continue to receive generous taxpayer-funded pensions. Many, having time on their hands, will take up part-time jobs. They will be able and prepared to accept low wages and will threaten still further the financial security of many, particularly the self-employed.)

When Labour came to power in 1997, England's pension system was in good condition. The State pension system was affordable and one of the best in the world. Pensioners' incomes had risen faster than wages. Britons had more money saved for their old age than citizens of any other EU country and, possibly, any other country in the world.

But things have changed for the worse.

The nation's pension fund is actually a huge debt. The national insurance you pay isn't insurance at all. It's just another tax. The money you pay into a Government sponsored scheme so that you will have an enhanced state pension isn't a pension contribution at all. It's just another tax, which goes into the pot to pay for the wages and pensions of nearly six million civil servants, one million unemployed, three million long-term sick and millions of pensioners. The money you think you're paying towards your state pension isn't being put on one side for your retirement. It is being used to pay today's bills. The Government is running an entirely fraudulent pension scheme. If the Government was a pension company all the directors would be in prison. It's hardly surprising that the Labour Government has warned that people will, in future, have to work until they are 70 or even longer, before they can receive a state pension. (Unless they work for the Government, of course. Firemen can start drawing their pensions at the age of 50. Policeman can retire at 55. Civil service bureaucrats can retire on a full pension at 60. And politicians can retire whenever they want.)

Non-Government employees who retire in a decade or two (and who rely on the state pension) will, if we remain in the

EU, receive less from their Government than citizens of any other EU country. Those Britons who rely on Government pensions in 20 or 30 years time will live in poverty. England's pension system is in a mess. Labour has turned one of the best pensions systems in Europe (and the world) into one of the worst. A survey by the Clydesdale Bank found that of 1,000 people questioned over 600 said they hoped to win the lottery to pay for their retirement.

Private pensions are in as big a mess as the State's own fraudulent pension scheme.

Liabilities have rocketed and assets have shrunk. Schemes that were well funded less than a decade ago are now in deficit. In a vast variety of private pension schemes there are huge gaps between the value of pension assets and the value of pension liabilities. The safety and security of corporate schemes, once taken for granted, is now questionable. The value of private schemes is widely doubted. Trust has gone.

There are several reasons for the mess.

First, the collapse of the stock market in the year 2000 destroyed much pension fund value. But this is something that happens from time to time. And those who invest in pensions have had to face this problem ever since pensions were first devised. The difference this time was that a great many company pension schemes were over-invested in (and over-exposed to) the stock market.

Most companies had their funds largely invested in fairly high risk equities in the hope that the bull market of the 90s would continue for ever, thereby ensuring that the company pension fund didn't need topping up with company money. Sadly, although equities can be profitable they can, when the market goes in the other direction, result in huge losses. Forcing public and private companies to provide pensions for their employees was a fundamental error. Labour, obsessed with taking authority but passing on responsibility, has made things infinitely worse through its introduction of compulsory stakeholder pensions. Occupational pension schemes in England are, according to one investment bank, now underfunded by £54 billion. This means that hundreds of big companies have huge debts to their own pension funds. These debts will be a burden on growth, investment and dividends and will help to hold back the stock markets (and therefore damage pension funds still further) in the future.

Many large companies are now working not to earn money for their shareholders but to earn money to pay today's and tomorrow's pensioners. Many big companies are now effectively hedge funds, running a business on the side. The trouble is that the people running the 'hedge fund' really don't have the foggiest idea what they are doing. In many cases the company pension scheme is bigger than the business and in numerous cases the pension fund's deficit is far greater than the company's assets. You may think your firm is an airline or a telecommunications company but in reality it is probably an investment company – heavily invested in, and dependent upon, retailers, mining companies and other airlines or telecommunications companies.

It isn't possible, by the way, to avoid this problem by investing overseas for the pensions problem is also affecting other countries. In the USA, General Motors, the world's biggest company, now only has one active worker for every 2.5 retired ex-workers receiving a pension. The fixed cost of paying pensions to 420,000 former workers is rapidly destroying the company. Providing health care insurance costs another $5 to £6 billion a year. It is hardly surprising to discover that a decade ago the non-executive chairman of General Motors announced that the main role of the company's Chief Executive Officer was not to boost the share price or increase shareholder value but simply to 'sustain the enterprise'. As *Fortune* magazine concluded, the implication was that General Motors true mission is 'to provide jobs for its employees, business for its suppliers, cars for its dealers, and pensions for its retirees'. Hardly a sound investment for shareholders.

Second, the Labour Government has introduced a bizarre pensions credit system which actively discourages saving. Obsessed with means testing, Labour politicians have introduced a form of means testing for pensions which means that those who spend their money are better off than those who bother saving. (It has to be said that means-tested pension plans are deliberately so complex that only the long-term unemployed – traditional users and abusers of the system – know how to use them properly. Nearly two million of the poorest pensioners do not claim their entitlement.) Is it any wonder that most people don't bother to save anything? Even non-pension savings have taken a dive. The English now save less than 5% of their income – less than half the amount saved by the French, the Germans and those devil-may-care spendthrifts, the Italians.)

Third, a surprising number of pension scheme managers turned out to be incompetent or devious and the Government's own watchdogs turned out to be toothless and unable or unwilling to bark out warnings. Three of the safest investments at the turn of the millennium were Equitable Life, zero dividend preference shares and Railtrack. Much of the money entrusted to Equitable Life was lost through the incompetence of those managing the company. Publicity about the Government's theft of Railtrack and the fraud (inspired by traditional, old-fashioned greed and dishonesty) which robbed investors in safe zero dividend shares of millions of pounds of their savings all damaged the enthusiasm of savers.

The Government did nothing to prevent these disasters (though it should and could have done) and it has, subsequently, done nothing to compensate those who lost their savings (though it should have done since the companies involved were all regulated by Government watchdogs paid for by investors and taxpayers). The Government regulators and watchdogs (the ones which imperil your personal financial security by pressuring banks to insist that you entrust your passport, your driving licence, your latest bank statement and a selection of gas bills to the post if you want to open a new bank account) did nothing to stop these thefts and frauds.

It is hardly surprising that a recent survey showed that 34% of adults are failing to save *anything* for their future. Since a growing number of young people are, in the future, also going to have to pay off student loans (together with the interest, of course) this situation seems certain to deteriorate. The number of people in serious debt and the number filing for bankruptcy have both reached record levels. Even people who have a little money don't trust anyone in the financial industry to handle it for them.

But it is the fourth and final reason which is really behind the crisis.

In his very first budget in 1997, within days of taking over the chauffeur driven car, the Chancellor of the Exchequer, Gordon Brown, introduced a tax change which took £5 billion a year out of private pension funds. This raid on the funds of people who had been foolish enough to save for their retirement was hailed by Labour's enthusiastic supporters as a clever way to raise more money to pay for more public sector jobs for Labour voters, but at the time I wrote an article pointing out that the new tax would decimate pensions and create a crisis. That is, I'm afraid, exactly what has happened.

It was Brown's mean tax-grab which has destroyed private pensions and created a huge disparity between those who will rely for their pensions on corporate or private schemes and those who work for the Government and whose guaranteed, index linked pensions will be paid by future taxpayers.

Brown's tax-grab effectively divided the nation into two. Between 1997 and 2005 Brown took £40 billion out of private pension funds. That is a large part of the current shortfall. Labour's crude and selfish policy was to buy votes with money taken from pensions. At the time most commentators were desperately in love with Blair, Brown and the Labour trickery and were far too stupid to see the possible consequences. I believe that Brown, who likes voters to think of him as 'prudent', has seriously damaged the pensions of far more people than Robert Maxwell, and has done far more damage to the enthusiasm of citizens for contributing to their pensions than Maxwell ever did. Brown's legacy will be several generations of impoverished people. So much for prudence.

The Government's failure to protect investors, its failure to compensate those who invested and were cheated out of their savings, its greedy grab at private and corporate pension funds and its introduction of a nasty form of means testing designed to punish those who have been prudent and have saved and reward those who have no savings, all mean that it is hardly surprising that people are no longer saving for their old age. The Government has told people that it is foolish to be prudent, and people have listened. Savers have become spenders.

As I have already suggested, the only people with really reliable pensions are the people who work in or for the Government.

MPs recently voted themselves a 25% increase in their pensions. When they discovered a £25 million black hole in their retirement fund they simply filled it in with taxpayers' money. Simple. MPs, like the army of Government employees hired to ensure that Labour stays in power, have copper-bottomed index-linked futures. Greed and theft and dishonesty are the principles upon which Blair and his chums run the country. When Blair's old chum Derry 'wallpaper' Irvine left office he did so with a taxpayer-funded pension pot worth £2.3 million. If you or I managed to save that much in our pension pots we would be penalised by the Inland Revenue because the limit for citizens who aren't Blair's chums is £1.5 million. Two lawyers drew up a scheme to exempt senior judges from the ceiling on tax exempt pension savings. The two lawyers were the Prime Minister and his former flat mate, Lord Falconer.

(No one has yet explained why the Government's scheme to punish (with extra taxes) private pension holders who save hard and accumulate more than £1.5 million in their pension funds, but to exempt civil servants and politicians who have more than £1.5 million of public money in their pension pots, is not in breach of that part of the Human Rights Act which decrees that all citizens must be treated equally.)

It is, perhaps, not surprising that in April 2005 (when the Association of British Insurers reported that 87% of the working population said they did not trust the Government not to let them down on pensions) the then pensions minister, said he did not think that England had a pensions crisis. This was true enough for State employees in general. And it was particularly true for a man who had a generous, guaranteed index-linked pension, paid for by taxpayers.

The pensions of MPs, judges, and senior civil servants are all guaranteed by the taxpayer. Moreover, the pensions of the nation's leaders are index-linked (at tax payers' expense). At a time when most privately employed citizens can no longer afford decent pensions (and are banned by the 2006 pensions legislation from putting as much into their pension funds as they might wish) it is a brutal scandal that judges and politicians should award themselves such generous pensions. It is yet another example of the new class system which Labour has created.

The potential cost of providing pensions for an ever-increasing number of State employees is rocketing.

State employees get their pensions from a Government sponsored Ponzi scheme. Their pensions are underwritten by taxpayers but unlike private pensions (where the contributions must be put into an invested fund) State employees get their pensions out of that year's tax revenue. The growing number of State employees, and the growing size of all those index-linked pensions, means that taxes are going to have to rise, rise and rise again. Private sector employees, whose own pensions have been destroyed by the Government's tax grab, and whose own futures are dim, are hardly likely to be pleased at the prospect of paying ever higher tax bills so that traffic policemen, tax collectors and incompetent Government ministers can be maintained in luxury in their retirement.

Workers who are employed by the state receive pensions which are, on average, 20% higher than people working for private companies. The public sector pensions bill costs taxpayers around £18 billion a year and to fund the pensions of current state workers and those already retired will cost £580 billion.

How would you feel if you were told that you had to find £10,000, walk into a Government building and hand it to a civil servant for his personal use?

Whether you work for the Government or not, the amount you will have to pay for the pensions of Government employees is around £10,000. You will, of course, also have to find the money to finance your own pension. And Government employees will not be supporting you.

The cost of funding over-generous pensions for state employees is one of the reasons for ever rising taxes. It is also one of the reasons why local authorities are charging ever higher rates and providing constantly deteriorating services.

In April 2005, local authorities in England and Wales revealed a £30 billion black hole in their pension funds. The deficit has risen dramatically in the last few years (it was a relatively small £6.3 billion just four years earlier) and seems certain to continue to rise at a frightening rate. Local authority employees simply threaten industrial action every time politicians hint that some sort of action will need to be taken to limit a system of accounting that would have had Mr Micawber weeping. In 2004 around a fifth of all the money raised by local councils as rates payments was paid directly into pension funds.

If your annual rate bill is £1,000 this means you are paying £200 of your own after-tax income towards the pensions of former council workers. Even if the situation remained stable it would take local authorities around 21 years to make up their pension deficits out of income. Since the situation isn't going to remain stable (it is deteriorating rapidly) it is patently clear that the future for rate payers is bleak. (Bizarrely, and almost unbelievably, many councils are deliberately making things worse for their ratepayers. More than 90 councils have now set up new pension schemes for their councillors. There was a time when councillors regarded their work as a civic duty and a privilege. Today, it is increasingly regarded as yet another well-paid branch of politics. The provision of pensions for councillors can only deepen the coming pensions crisis in local government.)

In early 2005, the Labour Party announced plans to raise the minimum retirement age for local authority workers from 50 to 55 but backed down after five unions threatened to go on strike to defend the present system. There is something quite cruel about a situation which allows council workers to retire at 50 (paid by tax payers) while tax and rate paying employees with private pensions (paid out of their own savings) or tax and rate paying employees retiring on state pensions (paid by tax payers) are being told by the Government that they must work well into their 70s before they can expect to retire.

What has all this got to do with the EU? Read on.

# 186

A few years ago European governments were telling young couples to limit the size of their families. There was much concern about Europe becoming overpopulated.

How things have changed.

Today, governments throughout Europe are encouraging women to have more babies.

Why?

The reason is simple.

The Ponzi schemes which governments run (and which they call their pensions programmes) are running out of time. Populations are getting older, the number of people who can't or won't work is rising and the percentage of the population working for, or otherwise relying on governments for their income, is increasing rapidly. The amount of money governments are paying out in pension payments will soon exceed the amount they are taking in from taxpayers.

You don't need to be a financial genius to work out that EU policies (supported and endorsed by the English Government) mean that we're heading for serious problems.

The EU's only way of holding off chaos for another few years is to dramatically increase the number of young people in Europe.

There are only two ways to do that.

The obvious, quick solution is to encourage immigration. So-called 'asylum seekers' fit this bill perfectly. (There is more about this later in this book.)

I say 'so-called' because the phrase 'asylum seeker' suggests that someone is escaping from a threatening, totalitarian regime. The phrase would, I suggest, be more accurately applied to the hundreds of thousands of middle-class Britons currently leaving England than to the hundreds of thousands of immigrants moving in.

The other solution is to encourage women to have more babies. Loads of babies.

With the help of the EU, the Labour Government has already tried to do this by a massive piece of social engineering designed to penalise taxpayers who don't have children.

♦ They have introduced absurdly over-generous programmes of maternity and paternity leave. (The scheme has back-fired to a certain extent because thousands of employers are now wary about hiring young women of child-bearing age.)

♦ They have introduced a means-tested scheme enabling parents to claim chunks of money just for having children. (This scheme is so absurd that even couples earning over £60,000 can claim the hand-out.)

♦ They have dramatically improved the quality and availability and accessibility of child care so that young mothers can have loads of children and still go out to work.

♦ They have devised a bizarre scheme of benefits which encourages teenage girls to have as many babies as they like. The State pays them and provides them with housing. It can be no surprise that pregnancy is now seen by many teenage girls as a career path. In effect the State has turned into a giant pimp: encouraging young girls to have sex and become pregnant in the (probably vain) hope that their children will grow up to be productive tax-paying members of society.

This final scheme enables the Government to encourage population growth without there being any conflict with the official policy of discouraging marriage – an institution which has never been favoured by statists who believe that the institution must always take precedence over the individual. It is much easier to control a population when you break down family units. The result, of course, is that people who live on state benefits have more children so that they can claim the extra money whereas couples who work cannot afford to have more than one or two children because of all the taxes they pay. The Government has not yet realised that when a child grows up in a (probably one parent) family where there is no working parent the chances are high that the child will follow the same parasitical path when it reaches adulthood.

The EU, and the English Government, are guilty of massive (and appallingly incompetent) social engineering.

Indeed, their hubris and determination to interfere seems to know no bounds. Before the 2005 election, Labour announced that the 'first few months are so important in the life-chances' of children (the politicians presumably have access to information denied to the medical profession) that the Government must take responsibility for providing 'learning experiences' in the cot.

I'd like to think I dreamt that last bit.

But, sadly, I didn't.

# 187

The mass of people in England just want to get on with their lives. They want to live in a safe, secure environment with a decent infrastructure run efficiently and economically by the government. They want to be treated with respect and possibly even with compassion. And they want to be left alone as much as possible, free of unnecessary interference from the State. They would like to leave complex geo-political issues to the experts.

But just look at the calibre of people who are running things. Prescott. Brown. Straw. Blunkett. Byers. Blair. These people are not experts. Could any of these buffoons run a corner shop successfully? They seem to be driven not by a great desire to defend and protect England and its inhabitants (many Labour Ministers are Scottish and it has to be remembered that a high percentage of Scottish politicians hate the English and believe that they have a duty and a responsibility to avenge past defeats) but by a burning desire to better themselves. They are professional politicians. The first of an unpleasant breed of thick-skinned, insensitive men and women who are in politics because they weren't good enough to succeed in proper jobs.

Never, in our history, has the country been run by people with such little knowledge, such little inspiration and such little genuine passion. We are being managed by men and women who would be stretched to serve as councillors; men and women who would have risen far above their potential and capability if they had been pressed into running a parish hall.

## 188

The Nice Treaty (which was approved without English citizens having a chance to express their views on it) made it possible for the EU to ban political parties which are not approved by the EU.

## 189

*'The State' may come to mean no more than a self-elected political party, and oligarchy and privilege can return, based on power rather than on money.'*
GEORGE ORWELL *(THE LION AND THE UNICORN)*

## 190

The EU is taking away our privacy, our freedom, our culture, our history, our independence, our traditional rights and our security.

The bureaucrats in Brussels have made criminals of millions of previously law abiding citizens. For example, the number of EU laws regulating small businesses mean that most honest, hard-working, well-intentioned businessmen break the law on a daily basis and their chances of getting away with their 'crimes' are low. Honest, law abiding citizens are easier to 'catch' and easier to punish (usually with fines).

In contrast, real criminals have never had it so good.

In England today just one in 35 serious offences result in the culprit being caught and punished. Put another way, that means that 34 out of every 35 serious offences go unpunished. If you recognise that a huge number of crimes are committed by idiots it seems clear that committing a serious crime is now a pretty risk-free business. The police, like everyone else, are hamstrung by EU laws which give the criminals more and more rights and which force the police to spend an increasing amount of their time filling in forms and making sure that they do not offend our politically correct masters in Brussels.

The situation is now so bad in England that most people no longer bother to report crimes. The chances of getting the police to respond at all are poor, the chances of their catching the criminals are appallingly low and if you claim on your insurance the company involved will doubtless put up your annual premiums by the value of the claim. Naturally, the politicians can use this as evidence that people are content with their lot, whereas in fact everyone who isn't a leading politician or a judge (and who does not, therefore, have a policeman standing outside their home) knows that things are getting worse.

The lesson is clear: in the EU crime pays but hard work doesn't.

## 191

I have for many years argued that companies are amoral, and have agendas and requirements of their own.

My thesis, first put forward in my book *Toxic Stress* in 1991 and extended in the original version of *Animal Rights Human Wrongs* in 1999, has now been widely adopted (it was apparently used as a starting point for the film *The Corporation*). The argument is that the directors and executives of big companies have no control over the companies for which they work because it is the company's needs which must always come first.

The Company needs to make quarterly profits to satisfy corporate analysts. The Company needs to produce rising dividends in order to satisfy shareholders. The employees, however elevated and well rewarded they may be, are there simply to ensure that the company's needs are met. The modern company is a bit like the man-eating plant in the spoof version of *The Little Shop of Horrors*. It is never satisfied, can never be satisfied, and is unconcerned with the well-being of the humans who work for it or tend to its needs.

In an utterly misguided attempt to deal with this problem the rather simple-minded bureaucrats who run the European Union (and, therefore, our lives) have spent several decades attempting to control modern companies and turn them into socially responsible entities.

In this fruitless and destructive endeavour they have been supported by successive European governments who have spotted the financial advantages of heaping many of the State's responsibilities onto corporate structures.

Because very few (if any) bureaucrats or politicians have any real commercial experience (or, indeed, any experience of what life is like in the real world) they have done some pretty staggering (and probably irreversible) damage to the competitiveness of European companies.

Today, in rather pathetic attempts to keep the EU happy, even modestly sized companies employ Corporate Social Responsibility Officers, maintain CSR Departments, promote their CSR initiatives and spend fortunes on hiring CSR consultants.

Vast amounts of time, energy and money are wasted on pointless exercises in corporate political correctness.

In England, the Government forces companies to use their payrolls to perform 23 jobs which should be done by the Government. (When Labour came to power in 1997 the figure was 15.)

These delegated jobs include doling out maternity pay and tax credits and collecting fines and student loan repayments.

It is hardly surprising that the incidence of bankruptcy among small businesses (particularly those which are labour intensive) has reached record levels.

I don't think there is much doubt that one of the reasons

for the success of companies in China and India (and for the decline of European industries) is the enthusiasm of EU bureaucrats for interfering with the way companies are run, for forcing companies to take on numerous responsibilities which should be managed by the State (arranging pensions and organising social security payments are among the relatively few valid responsibilities of the State) and insisting that companies become 'socially responsible'.

The small tragedy is that by forcing companies to take on inappropriate and pointless responsibilities the EU bureaucrats have simply provided the slaves of the corporation (from the directors and the executives downwards) with a neat cop-out.

If corporations pay lip service to the bureaucratic requirements of the EU then the EU will leave them alone.

The big tragedy is that by forcing corporations to take on responsibilities for which they are not designed or well suited, the EU bureaucrats have done lasting and severe damage to the efficiency and effectiveness of European companies and to the employment prospects of millions of European workers who must rely for their livelihoods on corporate employment.

It is largely thanks to the EU that many European companies are now closing local plants, sacking their workers and moving their production, or their services, to another continent. China and India are gobbling up the work.

It is largely thanks to the EU, a series of incompetent governments and the witless greed of Labour stealing £5 billion a year from English pension funds, that many large companies are now so burdened with their pension responsibilities that they can no longer function as companies operating in their own area of expertise but are effectively no more than investment funds managing the company pension scheme.

The truth which EU bureaucrats have failed to spot (because of their ignorance of the way things work in the real world) is that corporations have no social responsibility other than making the maximum possible profits for their shareholders. That is why companies exist. It is all they exist for.

It was Adam Smith, the author of *The Wealth of Nations*, who first pointed out that: 'It is not from the benevolence of the butcher, the brewer, or the baker, that we expect our dinner but from their regard to their own interest.'

(I doubt if Smith was the first to realise this truth, but he was the first to express it so neatly and so he is entitled to the credit.)

Self-interest is the reason why capitalism works.

Investors put their money into companies not out of a sense of public service but so that they will receive a return. Employees go to work not through altruism but so that they will be able to feed, clothe, house and entertain themselves and their families. Self-interest is the very basis of our society.

And what is true for bakers and shoemakers is equally true for companies making bread and companies making shoes.

The company which makes a profit will serve its shareholders and its employees well.

It is the role of Government to prevent corporate excess and corporate crime. It is the role of Government to introduce legislation which will effectively control companies and make sure that they earn their money without damaging individuals or society. And it is the role of Government to introduce penalties and sanctions which ensure that just laws are obeyed and, most important of all, that it is in the interests of the company that the laws are obeyed.

The politicians of Labour and the bureaucrats of Brussels simply don't understand this.

And it is another reason why their project is failing.

## 192

Gordon Brown claims that the English economy is booming and that England has never been in better financial health. Really. You may not have read (because 'they' don't want you to) but in May 2005 personal bankruptcies were at a record high (more than a fifth higher than they were during their previous peak in the early 1990s when the English economy was emerging from recession). Most of those seeking the protection of bankruptcy are under 30 years old. They have been misled by the Labour Party's promises of eternal prosperity and have borrowed too much. Moreover, the number of mortgage repossessions was also at a record high in mid 2005. And remember that the burden of student loans hasn't yet begun to kick in.

We have, like our own EU-controlled Government (and like the Americans) become a nation of borrowers; financing our illusory prosperity with loans which we cannot afford.

## 193

The English Home Office predicted that 13,000 people from the eight former Soviet bloc countries which joined the EU in May 2004 would move to England. The Home Office got it wrong (as usual). In fact, more than 176,000 East Europeans arrived in England in the year following the controversial expansion of the EU. (The figure of 176,000 is the official figure. The real figure will be more than this, a lot more than this or a massive amount more than this.) Around 100,000 came from Poland.

The Home Office also predicted that after the initial 13,000 immigrants had arrived from the Soviet bloc countries the influx of new residents would fall off. Once again they were wrong. Official figures show that the number of East Europeans still arriving in the UK in the summer of 2005 was running at between 13,000 and 14,000 a month. That's as many new residents each month as the Home Office predicted would arrive altogether.

The Home Office has also estimated that an additional 60,000 arrived illegally before May 2004. Since they had arrived illegally they could not, of course, work legally or pay income tax.

Is it any wonder that our crowded roads are getting ever more crowded and that hospital waiting lists are getting longer by the week?

Why haven't the Home Office civil servants who were responsible for this massive underestimate been sacked? Anyone with a real job who made an error of such magnitude would be invited to spend more time with his or her family. But English civil servants never take responsibility for their cock-ups. The idiots responsible for this particular variety of chaos are doubtless looking forward to index-linked pensions (paid for by taxpayers) and knighthoods.

## 194

The malignant influence of the EU gets everywhere these days.

It is undoubtedly a result of our Government's craven obedience to the EU that the 'how to be British' curriculum designed for immigrants who want UK citizenship teaches little or nothing about English history.

Immigrants who want to be English must show that they know: their rights as EU citizens, how to obtain legal aid, how to use legislation designed to outlaw discrimination, how to claim unemployment benefits, how to seek compensation for unfair dismissal, how to complain about police conduct, how to complain about sexual harassment and details of the minimum wage and holiday pay. They must also show a working knowledge of how Brussels institutions operate.

There is, however, no need for would-be Britons to know anything about the Norman Conquest, the First World War, the Battle of Britain, Winston Churchill, Henry VIII, the English Civil War, the Battle of Trafalgar, the British Empire, the formation of the English Parliament or the Battle of Waterloo.

## 195

The Labour Government which has misruled England since 1997 is keen on immigration for several reasons.

First, as I have already explained, the state pension scheme which the Government runs is a Ponzi scheme. If anyone else but the Government ran it they would be in prison. Many taxpayers assume that the money they hand over (in tax and national insurance payments) is put away in a safe place on their behalf (and possibly even invested for them) so that when they retire they can collect a pension which will, even if not generous enough to pay for Caribbean cruises, pay for the necessities of life. However, as I have been pointing out for several decades, that isn't the way the Government runs things. The money you hand over is not put on one side for you. Instead, it is used to pay pensions for today's pensioners. When you retire your pension will be paid by whoever is around and paying tax and national insurance at the time. It's an old-fashioned, simple financial scam: an illegal Ponzi scheme. Governments have recently started getting worried about this particular piece of financial sleight of hand because they have realised that when tomorrow comes there won't be enough taxpayers to pay out all the pensions. This is why the loathsome Blunkett warned English taxpayers not to expect the Government 'to dig them out of poverty in their old age'. The disgraced Blunkett, with apparent contempt for honest working people, ignores the fact that the money that *should* be used to 'dig them out of poverty' is their own and not the Government's. (Blunkett, of course, will receive a massive index-linked pension paid for by taxpayers.)

The Labour Government believes that expanding the EU

and encouraging immigration will get them out of the mess they and previous governments have created. They are wrong. The new countries which are joining the EU have low birth rates and their demographic structure is even less attractive than that of Western Europe. The enthusiasm for allowing Turkey into the EU is largely led by those who suspect that Turkey's younger population will help to delay the date at which Europe's ageing population becomes a real problem. (They don't seem unduly concerned about the fact that allowing Turkey into Europe will eventually change Europe from a predominantly Christian State to a predominantly Muslim State.) And, of course, this theory only works if all the young immigrants who are allowed into the country become contributors rather than takers; they have to become active, tax paying workers rather than people living on benefits.

Second, the Labour Government believes that if it lets lots of people come into the country (and gives them chunky handouts to welcome them to England) they will be so grateful that they will vote Labour for evermore.

Third, the aim is to water down the local population and to make sure that the English are soon in a minority, unable to make much of a fuss when their country disappears. As immigrants pour into England (and most of them stay in England, rather than moving to Scotland or Wales – both of which are at best unwelcoming and at worst downright hostile to the English, let alone to Romanians) the percentage of English voters who have heard of William Shakespeare and Winston Churchill will soon become a minority. The rest of the English, the proud middle classes, will have all tottered off to France or Spain, diluting the local populations there. This is, make no mistake about it, all part of a doomed plan to make sure that the United States of Europe can be created without any real protest.

## 196

The EU has become a self-serving industry which now needs to continue to exist simply in order to satisfy the employment needs of the over-paid, over-fed people who work for it. It is difficult to find an accurate figure for the tens of thousands of people whose monthly salary cheques, hefty expenses and huge pensions are paid by the EU but, to put the whole thing in perspective, it is worth noting that there are 20,000 registered lobbyists in Brussels. There are also 2,600 registered 'interest groups' promoting the needs of their branch of industry, and countless thousands of journalists both writing pamphlets for the EU and then rewriting the pamphlets for public consumption.

## 197

Membership of the EU brings only costs and commitments and regulations. There are no benefits. Contrary to official propaganda, membership of the EU makes England less competitive and it endangers English jobs. The EU gives us costly and damaging regulations, diminishes our ability to control immigration and reduces our freedom.

## 198

Back in 1984, Tory leader Margaret Thatcher (one of a series of Prime Ministers who have failed England by not extricating the nation from the EU) managed to negotiate a deal whereby two thirds of England's net contribution to EU spending (the amount by which our contribution exceeded our receipts) was returned. This was the famous rebate and is worth around £3,000,000,000 a year. The other EU members accepted that England should get a rebate because our efficient farmers benefit far less from the Common Agricultural Policy than do the farmers of other countries (such as France).

However, the new members of the EU weren't signatories to the Thatcher rebate deal and they want to gouge as much out of England as they can. Naturally, the original members of the EU will support their suggestion that the English rebate should end.

# 199

New EU legislation enables tax authorities in EU member states to share information, and an international task force (known as the Joint International Tax Shelter Information Centre) has been established to enable tax authorities in different countries to coordinate their findings about taxpayers. The Inland Revenue is now authorised by EU legislation to send the information it acquires about English taxpayers spontaneously to tax collectors everywhere. Similarly, tax collectors in other countries now send information about English citizens with accounts or homes abroad to the Inland Revenue.

Moreover, a meeting of EU finance ministers in September 2004 agreed to set up a working group to work out how best to achieve direct-tax harmonisation between EU member countries.

This is likely to lead to the EU replacing individual, national tax systems and replacing them with a single EU wide system. If it helps to avoid protests from nations worried about losing their sovereignty the EU will simply encourage individual nations to 'adjust' their tax rates to match general EU rates.

The English Government has, of course, stated firmly that it is firmly opposed to harmonisation of tax rates within the EU. However, as long as England remains a member of the EU the Government will have no authority to approve or oppose these changes.

# 200

All English firms are subjected to a flood of regulations from Brussels. But 91% of English firms do no trade whatsoever with other parts of the EU.

# 201

Before it was elected, in 1997, the Labour Party announced itself firmly against animal cruelty. Though this is now difficult to believe, it sold itself as the party for animal lovers. The oh-so-eager-to-be Prime Minister (who would have promised anything to get himself into Downing Street) announced, among other things, that he would call for a Royal Commission to investigate the scientific validity of vivisection.

Naturally, within weeks of being elected Blair & Co. had abandoned all this fluffy animal stuff. Scared of upsetting the international pharmaceutical industry they announced that there would be no Royal Commission on animal experiments after all. That, it was clear, had been simply a vote-catching ploy. The truth is that they couldn't possibly have a Royal Commission because they, the drug industry and everyone else, knew damned well that any independent enquiry would be bound to find that vivisection is not just worthless but that it actually endangers the lives of patients.

But, there was another problem Blair & Co. might well not have been aware of until they took possession of the large offices and the chauffeur-driven limousines.

The EU is an enthusiastic supporter of experiments on animals.

It is, indeed, currently planning one of the world's biggest and most entirely useless series of experiments.

Around 80,000 chemicals are currently in use by manufacturers. Chemicals are used in pesticides, solvents, packaging, cars, appliances, toys and foods (particularly meat).

Only 10,000 of this 80,000 have ever been tested for human health effects. Of these, 52 are known to cause cancer in humans and 176 are suspected of being carcinogens.

We simply don't know about the rest. No one has ever checked. Occasionally, it becomes clear that such and such a chemical or food constituent causes cancer. There is then a panic and all foods containing that chemical are removed from the shelves.

So now, under new legislation called REACH (Registration, Evaluation, Authorisation and Restriction of Chemicals), the EU is testing all chemicals on animals. (So too is the USA. The EU is doing one set of tests. America is doing another set of identical tests.)

This is a total, utter waste of time and money.

Countless millions of animals will die in vain.

Vivisection is a barbaric waste of time, of no value whatsoever to human beings.

# 202

There are many myths about animal experimentation.

Some supporters argue that attempts to bring animal experimentation to an end are doomed because animal experiments are regarded as essential by the law and, indeed, by the medical profession's own requirements.

In fact there are no laws in the UK requiring drug companies (or anyone else) to perform animal experiments (see my book *Fighting for Animals* for the evidence). The World Medical Association's Declaration of Helsinki (on recommendations guiding physicians in biomedical research in human subjects) was officially amended in 2000 and laboratory procedures on animals are no longer recommended as essential before studies in humans are conducted.

Animal experiments are conducted only because they enable drug companies to launch new products on the market without proper clinical testing.

The EU is testing tens of thousands of chemicals on animals because the chemical companies know they can't lose. If a test on an animal shows that a chemical causes cancer the test will be ignored on the grounds that animals and people are different. If a test on an animal shows that a chemical doesn't cause cancer in that animal the test will be used as proof that the chemical is safe. The EU is doing these tests because the chemical companies want them to do them.

How can I prove this?

Simple.

This is exactly what the drug companies have been doing for decades. (The evidence appeared in my book *Betrayal of Trust.*)

## 203

The real bottom line is stark: no animal experiment has ever saved a human life. But animal experiments have led to many human deaths. That's the truth and all the evidence supports it. But, as always, neither Labour nor the EU are interested in anything as boring and unprofitable as the truth. The EU's new animal testing policy is just another example of the EU responding to a real problem in an impractical way which benefits only those with a vested interest in protecting the present corrupt and dishonest system.

## 204

The news that scientists are planning to insert microchips into people has been received with enthusiasm by EU bureaucrats.

The uncritical enthusiasts for this latest miracle of the modern age point out that instead of having to carry around lots of pieces of plastic (credit cards, bank cash cards, membership cards and so on) we can all have a single microchip stuck under the skin on our arms.

It will be a case of 'chips in everyone'.

'Credit cards, bank cash cards – all redundant!' said one EU supporter to whom I spoke. He was positively aglow with enthusiasm. 'Every bit of information you need to carry around with you will be on your own personal microchip. If you want to get cash out of a bank you just stick your arm into a hole in the wall. The bank's scanner will check your microchip and then, if you've got enough money in your account, simply dispense the cash!'

'It sounds very convenient,' I said, extremely cautiously. The alarm bells were already beginning to ring.

'Never again will anyone have to worry about having their credit cards stolen!' said the enthusiast for all things new.

'Ruthless thieves might just chop off people's arms,' I pointed out.

'Oh come on! Don't make fun!' protested the enthusiast rather crossly. 'This is a serious breakthrough which is going to revolutionise people's lives. No more money belts when travelling abroad, no more credit card insurance. No more worry about what to do with your wallet when you go for a swim. No need to carry cash around with you at all. Every shop, every hotel, every petrol station will have a machine to read your arm.'

I told the europhile that I agreed that this would in some ways be extremely handy.

'What's more,' said the enthusiast, ignoring the pun, 'personal information can be stored on the same microchip.'

'What sort of personal information?' I asked, suspiciously.

'Birth date, driving licence details, passport number, income tax records, national insurance number,' said he. 'Just imagine! You could travel abroad without worrying about whether or not you had your passport with you. And you could even have details of your airline bookings recorded on your microchip. You could walk through customs in your bathing costume! There would be no need to carry a fistful of documents with you. It would be easy to put in voting registration details too!'

When you visited your local polling station you'd just stick your arm into the box and vote. What's more, confidential medical information could be stored on the same microchip!'

I looked at him. 'Medical information?'

'The way things are at the moment the chances are that some of your medical records are stored with your general practitioner and some with whichever hospital consultant you've been seeing. This new system will mean that any doctor you see will have instant access to all your medical notes! And if you change doctors there will be no long delay while your medical records follow you. If you are knocked down in an accident the casualty doctors who look after you will simply stick your arm into a machine and find out what drugs you're taking, what allergies you have, whether you are diabetic, epileptic or whatever else!'

'How feasible is all this?' I asked the EU fan.

'Oh it's entirely possible now,' he replied. 'Tests are underway and schemes like this will be available to the public very shortly.'

'And I bet the authorities will be very enthusiastic,' I said. 'People who agree to have the microchips implanted will probably get tax rebates.'

'Absolutely! Splendid idea. That would be a great encouragement.'

'Presumably these microchips use the same sort of technology as the subscriber cards used by satellite television?'

'I think so.'

'That's interesting,' I said. 'If you have trouble with your subscriber card and want to have a channel unscrambled, you just telephone the company. They will then send a message to your card to unscramble the channel.'

'Yes?' said the EU supporter, obviously not quite understanding what I was getting at.

'They can send a message through the air directly to your own very personal subscriber card,' I pointed out.

'Yes,' he agreed. 'It's very quick and very convenient.'

'And so what is there to stop the authorities sending messages to the microchip implanted under the skin of your arm?'

'I don't see what you're getting at.'

'The authorities will be able to edit the information on your microchip any time they want to. They can not only find out anything they want to know about you but they can also cancel your passport, your driving licence and your bank card whenever they like.'

'So?'

'In a perfect world where bureaucratic errors were unknown and bullying governments didn't exist it *might* be OK,' I said. 'But we don't live in a perfect world. We live in the EU.'

'You're paranoid.'

'They could decide how they wanted you to vote. And make sure that you voted in the approved manner. If you complained or protested or caused a lot of trouble they could turn you into a non-person in seconds.'

'Don't be so silly!'

'And what about errors?' I asked. 'At the moment if one doctor makes an error when putting something into your medical records there is a chance – albeit a slim one – that another doctor might spot the error. And you can, of course, always ask to see your own medical records to check that everything they contain is fair and accurate. I suspect that open access will become a thing of the past when medical records are hidden away on a microchip underneath your skin. The non-availability of open access will simply mean that it will become even more difficult than it is at the moment for an ordinary citizen to check what the experts have written about him or her.'

The EU supporter frowned for a moment Then he brightened. 'I'm sure everything will be fine,' he said. 'We can trust the people in Brussels.'

# 205

Most of the members of parliament we have now will not rescue us from the EU.

Theoretically and historically, MPs are there to represent and protect the interests of their constituents. But today their main function is to act as lobby fodder for the party leadership, to be fed into the lobbies and counted.

If an MP's party is not in Government he or she has no power. If his or her party is in Government the amount of power they have depends on their influence with the leader (i.e. were they at school with him, have they ever shared a flat with him and so on).

In practise, the average MP who sits for one of the big three parties is representing not his constituents, the people who voted for him, but the party machine which selected him to represent the party at an election.

Most MPs are merely bit part actors, fit to open fetes, kiss babies and write patronising, self-glorifying rubbish for the local newspaper.

As I have explained before, I believe that we can change the way our nation is governed by voting not for candidates who represent the three big parties but by voting for candidates who represent smaller parties or (better still) stand as true independents.

Independent MPs have an enormous amount of power in the House of Commons. They can do a great deal of good for their local constituents. The vote of an independent MP cannot be relied upon by a big party machine. An honest and independent MP cannot be told to vote one way or the other. He cannot be threatened with expulsion from the party or bribed with a promise of minor office or a peerage. The independent MP must truly represent the interests of the people who sent him to Parliament. If he doesn't they won't vote for him again. The independent MP can demand things for his constituency and have a reasonable hope that his demands will be met. He will, at the very least, have a much greater hope of success than the MP who represents a party – whether that party be in or out of power.

And so at each and every forthcoming election vote for anyone whom you think might be able to defeat the Labour, Conservative and Liberal candidates.

If you think the Monster Raving Loony Party candidate might win – vote for him. If you think the Welsh Nationalist might win – vote for her. If you think the Green Party candidate might win – vote for him. If you think the BNP candidate might win – vote for her. If you think the UKIP candidate might win – vote for him.

That's real tactical voting. And it will give us back our Parliament and our country.

# 206

Around the 17th century, Europe became the most ambitious, most successful and richest area of the world. European countries stole, pillaged and conquered to win their wealth.

Then, in the early 20th century, the United States of America became the most powerful nation on earth. The USA stole, pillaged and conquered to gain its position.

Europe had several centuries of ascendancy and power. The USA will have had less than one century at the top because Asia (and in particular China and India) is where the future lies.

China and India already produce more engineers than does the USA. Chinese emigrants are now a powerful force even inside America. (Chinese is now the third most commonly spoken language in American homes, after English and Spanish, but very few Americans are bothering to learn it.)

In China, more than 40 million Chinese have driving licences and 40% of Chinese families are currently planning to buy their first cars. That's a lot of people and a lot of cars. It's also a lot of growth.

When each Chinese citizen consumes as much energy as American citizens do (which they soon will) China will use all the oil currently produced throughout the world.

When the Chinese produce as much carbon dioxide, per inhabitant, as the Americans do (which they soon will) then the global warming problem will be infinitely worse. (And the Americans, faced with global warming disasters of their own making will begin to wish they had been less selfish and more prepared to take action to deal with the problem.)

Meanwhile, as China grows and grows the EU, so self-assured, so full of itself, is a wounded beast, about to die. American and European students who used to complain about globalisation because they were worried about the growing power, and malevolent influence, of multinational corporations which originated in the west and obeyed no laws and paid no taxes, are now complaining about globalisation because they realise that most of the best jobs in the future will be confined to Asia.

## 207

For several years Europe has (like the USA) faced brutal competition from car manufacturers in Japan and Korea.

But instead of attempting to deal with the problem by looking for ways to improve productivity and efficiency the EU has destroyed Europe.

European firms are now uncompetitive because of the ruinous blizzard of regulations with which they have been showered by EU bureaucrats, themselves protected from the real world by their own secure contracts, their absurdly generous sickness schemes and their vastly over-generous pension programmes.

Bizarre working practices, over-protected workers, a 35 hour week, corporate pension schemes – all these things have helped to make Europe uncompetitive compared with Asia, and have helped to destroy European businesses.

177

And things are going to get worse. Much, much worse.

The European clothing industry has been moving manufacturing to China just as quickly as bosses can close down factories in Europe, and the EU has already been reduced to begging China to 'voluntarily' restrain its textile exports, claiming, rather pathetically, that if China doesn't stop exporting textile products to Europe there will be massive job losses in EU countries.

Not surprisingly, the Chinese Foreign Minister rejected this pathetic whinge as 'over-protectionist, irrational and unreasonable'. (If I complained to Rupert Murdoch that his ability to bulk buy gave him an unfair advantage, and that he was selling books too cheaply and damaging my business, do you think he would apologise and put up prices?)

The EU's request was particularly pointless for even if the Chinese had agreed to accommodate the European plea the manufacturing would have just gone to Thailand or Vietnam.

The truth is that China, an emerging power with very low labour costs, is now doing to Europe and America what Japan did a generation ago and what America did to Europe a century ago. (The Chinese are also stealing product designs in exactly the same way that Japan did a generation ago and America did over a century ago. However, the Chinese are not following the American example and patenting natural plants so that they can charge local populations hefty fees to use the naturally occurring products which they have been using for centuries.)

European manufacturers are at a disadvantage because of high wages, low working hours and low productivity and the influence of unions on working practices. But these are relatively minor problems compared to the problems created by EU bureaucracy.

## 208

The American Senate has voted to put a 27.5% tariff on all goods made in China – as if that will solve the problem. Some of the more bone-headed and arrogant Americans have even talked of using force to prevent China selling its products around the world. It is difficult to imagine anything more stupid than this.

China is far bigger than the USA and, unlike Iraq, is well-equipped with weapons of mass destruction. If it comes to a war the Chinese Government is unlikely to be worried by the loss of a few hundred thousand soldiers but just imagine the fuss in Washington, Chicago, Boston and Los Angeles if the American military had to justify sustaining losses of that magnitude.

(The Americans are so worried about the possibility of a conflict with China that war criminal Blair's best friend war criminal Bush has been leaning on the EU to drop their plans to start selling arms to China.)

## 209

Despite the fact that the European Union's exports to China have risen a staggering 600% in the last 15 years (you'd think we'd all be grateful) the EU is now so worried about China's ascendancy (the imports of Chinese-made bras and tights into the EU has gone up dramatically in recent years and seems to be a particular concern to the EU) that the bureaucrats have decided to introduce trade sanctions against China. The EU wants to follow America's example and put tariffs on imports from China.

The people who run the EU do not have the wit to realise that it is their incompetence, their appallingly stupid euro currency, their corruption and their mismanagement of the economy which has undermined European economies and has made European companies vulnerable to competition from India and China.

The morons at the EU seem to think the solution lies in *more* regulations. They are too stupid to realise that the solution lies in *less* regulations.

Introducing trade sanctions against China won't work. It is a juvenile, indefensibly protectionist, pointless response to a serious long-term problem. It's the sort of thing Americans do because their foreign policies are juvenile, indefensibly protectionist and generally pointless.

(America has maintained irresponsible and selfish fiscal policies for decades. American wealth is built on those irresponsible and selfish policies which have enabled it to steal billions from poor countries. America is awash with millionaires and billionaires but the money they have stashed away has been stolen at the expense of millions (and billions) of people living in poor countries. The Americans need to remember that China and India and other rapidly developing countries now hold billions of American dollars. If America starts a war against China (whether it be military or fiscal) it will lose.)

Attempting to tackle China by using trade quotas or tariffs is morally wrong (though I don't expect the word 'moral' is widely understood in Brussels) and pointless (something they definitely are familiar with). It is also the sort of typically woolly-headed thing that EU bureaucrats do.

But putting tariffs on Chinese goods won't work because the big advantage China has is that its people are ambitious and prepared to work long hard hours for very little money.

Inevitably, that makes Chinese goods very cheap.

# 210

Mr Zhang, The boss of Chinese appliance maker Haier, is in charge of 30,000 employees. The firm he runs is one of the biggest in the world. Mr Zhang is also an influential member of the Chinese Communist Party. And yet Mr Zhang earns about £450 a month and last year took home a bonus of considerably less than £2,000. Compare Mr Zhang to American style greed. When Jack Welch, the former boss of General Electric, retired he received a retirement package that can only be described as obscene. In addition to enough money to feed the payroll at a decent sized Chinese factory for years, Welch received a £50,000 a month apartment, free tickets to all the best sports events, use of the company's private jets and a regular supply of fresh flowers.

When the boss of one English company retired recently, not to tend to his roses but to take up another well-paid post, he was awarded a special payment of £250,000 for handing over to his successor. (Only after an enormous fuss did he eventually turn the payment down.)

## 211

In the long-term, the only way for European countries to survive is to find things they are good at, and to do them well. Meanwhile, in the short-term, countries in the EU would have a much better chance of surviving if the EU bureaucrats stopped producing red tape. It is the red tape which is suffocating businesses, creating unemployment and wrecking European prosperity.

But the EU bureaucrats aren't going to stop producing legislation. It is what they do. It is their *raison d'être*. In the end the EU will be killed by bureaucracy; strangled by the red tape produced by the unelected Brussels bureaucrats.

By leaving the EU, England will give herself a chance of surviving in a harsh new world.

If she remains in the EU England will, like the other EU member countries, be finished as an industrial nation and finished as a world force.

## 212

*'We are ruined by Chinese cheap labour.'*
BRET HARTE, 1870.

## 213

The bureaucrats of Brussels and the EC commissioners think they know all the answers but in reality they don't even know the questions. And they have lost the plot.

## 214

Anyone who is any doubt about the fact that the bureaucrats in Brussels are planning a European superstate need only look at the development of European 'agencies'.

There are now 10 EU agencies covering many different aspects of our lives. There are, for example, EU agencies controlling food, aviation safety and human rights.

These pan-European agencies (which were described in a White Paper on EU Governance in 2001) were set up to help organise a supranational system of government throughout Europe. The aim, quite simply, was to give the European Commission and its bureaucrats control over national civil servants in areas of policy and law enforcement. (The basic rule within the EU is that power can only ever be transmitted towards the centre of the EU.)

In particular, the EU, having spent 50 years creating tens of thousands of laws, wants to take control of law enforcement without having to put up with interference from democratically elected domestic politicians.

And so the EU has created a whole team of agencies designed to take power from national governments and their civil servants.

Local, national, civil servants (those working in London and Paris, for example) are now employed solely to ensure that the wishes of the EU's agencies are carried out.

The bill for creating and running all these agencies (which, naturally, runs into billions of pounds a year) will, until the EU has its own European tax collectors, be met by national taxpayers in each individual country. The agencies will be able to charge for their regulatory services. In other words we in England are paying the EU to run agencies to tell the civil servants in London (whose salaries and costs we also pay) what to do.

Businesses whose work brings them into contact with these agencies will have Kafkaesque experiences. Small businesses in particular, which do not have their own specialist translators and EU rule book interpreters, will find themselves spending days ringing bureaucrats in foreign agencies as they attempt to find out what they have to do to stay in business and out of prison.

I was recently sent technical documents in German which relate to my work as an author and publisher. Knowing that the English Government is always ready to spend its taxpayers' money on providing documents in whatever language is required I wrote and politely asked if I could have copies of the documents in English. I was told that I had to find a translator because the documents were only available in German.

Oh what fun the EU brings.

Anyone thinking of setting up a small business within the EU these days should be certified insane.

## 215

*'A really efficient totalitarian state would be one in which the all-powerful executive of political bosses and their army of managers control a servitude. To make them love it is the task assigned, in present day totalitarian states, to ministries of propaganda, newspaper editors and schoolteachers.'*
ALDOUS HUXLEY (*BRAVE NEW WORLD*)

# 216

Most small company bosses loathe the European Union. But multinational corporations (particularly American ones) are EU supporters.

Now, why on earth would that be?

The answer is simple.

Large companies are not as right wing as their critics often suggest. Large companies don't believe in free thinking, in free enterprise or, indeed, in free anything. But they do believe in dictatorship, a single world government and state socialism. At the two extremes there is no difference between the far left and the far right. It was, remember, the same few powerful companies and organisations which financed both Hitler and Stalin. (How many remnants of those same greedy vultures now control the EU I wonder?)

Statism (an updated version of communism) and state control suits the needs and interests of big corporations much better than the 'small is beautiful' philosophy. Allegedly left wing politicians (such as some members of the Labour Party) have a great deal in common with those who represent multinational corporations. Try defining the philosophical difference between the EU and a multinational and you'll see what I mean. It is, perhaps, not quite so surprising that their representatives enjoy each other's company in organisations such as the Bilderbergers.

It is the dislike of the 'small is beautiful' philosophy, and an affection for large, bureaucratic organisations which can be controlled more effectively, which has made the EU and the Labour Government conspire to banish almost every small and independent aspect of our lives.

Small hospitals, small medical centres with just two or three doctors working there, small post offices – all these are being banned. The EU and the Government want only large hospitals and super-surgeries with ten doctors and a team of full time administrators. These can be controlled far more efficiently, and can be fitted much more comfortably into the statist world of the all conquering European Union.

## 217

Private companies have at last realised that management consultancy is something of a fraud but the English Government is following the EU's example by wasting an increasing amount of taxpayers' money on hiring management advisors.

Vast quantities of money are now being spent on creating EU approved league tables and targets which are always met because the figures are spun (fiddled).

Management consultancy fees paid by the public sector almost doubled in 2003 and now top £1.3 billion a year.

There have for years been far too many managers in English industry. Now there are far too many managers in public sector areas too. Too many chiefs and not enough Indians. Astonishingly, there are now less than three employees for every manager in England.

England desperately needs less people giving orders and more people doing things. The NHS, for example, is now awash with highly paid managers who probably don't know the difference between a triangular bandage and a bedpan.

## 218

Since they came to power in 1997, Labour politicians have consistently promised to cut Government bureaucracy. Like all Labour promises this is, of course, just a lie. (Labour politicians spell 'promise' as a three letter word: 'l-i-e'.)

Today, the civil service, the health service, local councils, schools, colleges and universities, quangos and so on employ 7.4 million people. (By the time you read this the figure will doubtless be much higher.) These are, I stress, people employed by the nation rather than working for it. There is a difference.

Since Labour came to power in 1997 they have (despite their promises to cut staff and costs) added nearly a million people to public sector staff. And the hiring is increasing because it helps keep down unemployment figures and because most of those hired will vote for the Government which has given them a job.

Most of the people newly hired by Labour are paid to do what can best be described as non-jobs which contribute nothing to our society. Indeed, many have a powerful negative effect since they are employed to enact legislation produced by the EU. Local councils all over the country are now hiring 'five a day coordinators' to persuade people to eat more fruit, and 'real nappy officers' to persuade mothers to use old-fashioned nappies (a laudable aim, perhaps, but why do local councils need to use ratepayers' money to hire people to encourage this?).

On one typical day recently the *Guardian* (the Government's official job centre notice-board) had 124 pages of advertisements for jobs paying up to £150,000 a year. As an example, one advertisement for a job in the public health sector asked for someone to work as a 'smoking cessation adviser for adults and young people'. Applicants were assured that 'a lack of clinical knowledge will not be a disadvantage'. For this applicants were offered up to £24,424 a year.

It is in the Government's interests to keep hiring staff. But many of the people the Government is hiring with our money are being hired to satisfy the requirements of the EU. If we leave the EU our expenditure on worthless additions to the nation's payroll will plummet and we will all be far, far richer in every conceivable way.

## 219

Millions of workers in England are now aware of the effects of EU legislation. Vast numbers of employers now prefer to take on part-time or short-term contract employees for the simple reason that by doing this they can often avoid some of the EU legislation governing the way employees are treated.

The EU bureaucrats may have meant their legislation to improve the security of employees. In practice the EU legislation has dramatically *reduced* the security of employees.

## 220

Almost every important change in English law and culture for several decades has been a result of legislation demanded by unelected European bureaucrats and, tagged on almost as an irrelevant afterthought, a European Parliament which is to democracy what George Bush is to world peace. The EU now reaches, uninvited and unwanted, into every aspect of our lives.

For example, a trivial thing, but today, on my desk I have a note from the Driver and Vehicle Licensing Agency telling me that I am going to be given a new Vehicle Registration Certificate which 'has been developed to comply with a European Directive, which requires member states to introduce a common format for Registration Certificates'.

## 221

England's contribution to the EU budget is currently £9.5 billion. That is to say that every year we donate £9,500,000,000 to the European Union to do with as it will. The biggest recipients of EU largesse include Spain, which receives around £9.5 billion a year from the EU. What a surprise it was when the Spanish voted 'yes' to the new EU constitution. (The Spanish would have to be certifiable not to vote for an organisation which gives them £9.5 billion every year.)

If England leaves the EU, and we still feel a burning desire to give away vast shiploads of money, I'm sure the Spanish would accept an annual cheque for £9.5 billion from the Chancellor of the Exchequer – that way we would still be poorer and they would be richer but we would cut out the middlemen in Brussels.

## 222

It was George Orwell who pointed out that Hitler's Germany, in the guise of the Nazi Party, controlled investment, raw materials, rates of interest, working hours and wages and that although the factory owner still owned his factory he was for practical purposes reduced to the status of a manager. What difference is there between the EU and the Nazi Party?

## 223

Owners of cars which were no longer good enough to drive used to be able to sell them to scrap dealers. They would usually receive a few pounds for the wreck.

Today, thanks to new EU rules which define the ways in which cars can be scrapped, owners have to pay £100 to have an old car taken away.

The result is that a million cars will be abandoned in England in 2005. The bill for removing all these unwanted vehicles will run into hundreds of millions and will be paid by local authorities (and, therefore, by honest local ratepayers and by taxpayers).

# 224

It was the EU which was responsible for the daft rules which result in perfectly good furniture being thrown away if it doesn't have an EU acceptable fire certificate.

Theoretically, the legislation exists to save lives.

In practice the legislation simply results in a vast amount of wastage and hugely increased profits for the furniture making industry.

There are some who wonder if old furniture, which currently has to be dumped in landfill sites, could be made safe by spraying it with a fire retardant.

# 225

There are some subjects which are too important, too fundamental, for fence-sitting. You are either for hanging or not. You were either for the invasion of Iraq or you were not. The EU is one of those subjects. You are either for the EU or not.

# 226

The Labour Government in general, and John Prescott in particular, blame the shortage of affordable housing on house-builders who, say the Labour politicians, should have built more houses and should have kept the prices down.

Not surprisingly, the house-builders don't agree with this criticism.

And they have good reasons for their point of view.

There have, they point out, been lengthy delays in obtaining planning permissions. Many perfectly reasonable applications have been refused and red tape means that these days it takes up to 48 weeks to get a planning inspector to make a site visit. There is also a shortage of craftsmen. Misguided Government policies mean that the nation is awash with hairdressers and would-be television presenters but desperately short of bricklayers, carpenters, plasterers, electricians and plumbers.

But it is the new laws, regulations and rules (most of which were thought up in Brussels) which are really at the root of the problem. The EU and Labour have introduced an interminable host of new restrictions and building regulations (most of which have done nothing to make houses safer or better). All these new regulations have added enormously to the cost of building new houses and, therefore, to the cost of housing.

One building company, Taylor Woodrow, has reported that in 2004 it cost 60% more to build a house than it cost in 1997. And, they say, nearly half of that increase comes from new regulations.

Another house-builder claims that two fifths of the cost increase in house building since 1997 has come from additional building regulations and restrictions (many of them from the EU), very little of which adds to the value of homes or people's enjoyment of them. It is hardly surprising that whereas 425,000 houses were built in the UK in 1970, less than 180,000 were built in 2004.

If there is anyone to blame for the shortage of affordable housing there are only two culprits: the EU and the Labour Government.

Since the Labour Government has, on the whole, done nothing more than introduce regulations sent over from Brussels, it is the EU which is largely responsible for the current housing problem the nation faces.

Naturally, Labour Ministers refuse to acknowledge this pretty obvious cause-blame link. They do not dare to criticise the glorious new federal state of Europe – the fountain of such wealth for its bureaucrats and politicians.

Instead of cutting back on some of the more absurd regulations from Brussels, Labour is insisting that developers provide a number of affordable homes every time they apply for planning permission for a new housing estate. Naturally, this simply bumps up the cost of the rest of the development. It is a typically Statist solution.

## 227

Have you noticed how those three wonderful words 'Made In England' have disappeared? Today, all you are likely to see is a mark showing that the product was Made In Europe. (Actually, what you are more likely to see is 'Made In China'.)

## 228

Under EU rules, farmers in England are forbidden to produce as much milk as English citizens consume.

However, under EU rules farmers in France, Germany and Ireland can all produce more milk than their citizens use. The result of this is that English supermarkets are able to buy cheap milk from farmers in France, Germany and Ireland. As a result, the supermarkets are, of course, able to offer English farmers a knock down price for their milk.

Isn't life in the EU just wonderful?

## 229

The quality of education is falling dramatically throughout Europe as individual member countries of the EU struggle to cope with new regulations and the philosophy of political correctness espoused by the EU.

In France, when 15-year-olds were given a dictation test that had been passed by most pupils in 1988 they performed abysmally. More than half scored zero and 80% failed the test. After ten years of schooling more than half the pupils who leave school in France are still semi-literate and incapable of writing a letter or e-mail.

The same is true throughout the rest of the EU where cultural and intellectual values have been devastated in recent years.

In 2005, the head of Ofsted, the UK's schools watchdog, warned that the behavioural and verbal skills of children starting school were at an all time low and that some five-year-old children couldn't even speak properly. Standards of literacy have tumbled as school teachers have abandoned old-fashioned teaching methods which worked (but which were regarded as too tedious for teachers) in favour of new, politically correct systems which are useless.

Astonishingly, it isn't just in academic areas that school-children have been proved to be developing poorly.

English school teachers have admitted that they often have to teach children how to use a knife and fork in the school canteen and a survey by a restaurant chain showed that one in five children under the age of 11 usually eat all their food with their fingers.

Perhaps not all of this can be blamed on the EU. Other surveys have shown that 20% of families never have a sit down meal and 75% of the rest may be sitting down when they are eating their meals but they are also watching TV as they do so.

## 230

The EU Energy Commissioner has called for a 55 mph speed limit throughout Europe. The Commissioner seems to think that this will cut fuel consumption and save oil. Sadly, I fear he is mistaken. My car is fitted with a gauge which tells me how much fuel it is consuming and the gauge shows, quite clearly and consistently, that my car is more efficient at a higher speed and that, consequently, consumption is higher at 55 mph than it is at 70 mph. A 55 mph limit would, like so many other EU regulations, slow everyone down, waste time, damage the economy and cause boredom and accidents. It would also result in more fuel being used.

The one reliable thing about the EU, and its many well-paid representatives, is that it and they invariably manage to display a staggering level of stupidity and incompetence. Any business organisation which was as badly led and as grossly incompetent as the EU would have gone bankrupt years ago. (And its directors would by now be in prison.)

## 231

*'The officers of the new EU police force, Europol, are immune from criminal prosecution should they break the law while carrying out their activities.'*
ARTICLE 5, PARAGRAPH 2 OF THE EU COUNCIL ACT (1998)

## 232

As I explained in *England Our England,* Englishmen and women can now be extradited to any European country which is also a member of the EU. There is no right to trial by jury. The protection of habeas corpus (traditionally provided by English law) has gone.

One problem with this new EU law is that there are still many different laws in existing European countries. Activities which might be illegal in Greece or Romania may not be illegal in England. The extradition process was presumably introduced to help integrate former European nations into the United States of Europe. But it was introduced before the various countries had managed to integrate their legal systems. All Englishmen and women are now subject to all English laws, all EU laws and all the laws which may exist in other EU nations.

If you accidentally break a law when you are on holiday in Spain, and then return to England, the Spanish can demand that you be extradited and taken for trial in Spain. If you are at home in England, doing something on the Internet and you break a law in Germany then you can be extradited to

Germany for trial, sentence and punishment.

Anyone living in the EU who uses the Internet today should make sure that they are familiar with all the laws currently existing in their own country, with all the laws existing within the EU as a whole and all the laws existing in individual EU nations.

The only people exempt from the extradition law are German citizens.

Englishmen and women can be extradited to Germany.

But German men and women cannot be extradited to England.

(Oh, and if you are English you should remember that you are also subject to American law. Englishmen and women can now be extradited to the USA for trial if they are deemed to have broken American laws. Naturally, this law operates one-way only. Americans who break English laws cannot be extradited to England.)

## 233

Thanks to the EU, companies must ensure that at least 85% of their staff are able to cope with the demands of their jobs. Repetitive and boring jobs must be eliminated as far as possible. At least 85% of employees must have a say about the way they do their work – including some control over the pace at which they work and the timing of their breaks. And employees must be consulted on all changes, must be offered reasons for change and must be provided with a timetable.

It isn't difficult to tell that these regulations were thought up by bureaucrats who have never ever run a proper business – or even worked for one – but who work in a protected and cocooned environment where money is never a problem and work, which is something fitted in between breaks, consists of thinking up new rules which make their own lives better and better, without regard for others or for the community which pays them.

# 234

The EU and the English Government regard Israeli settlements in the territories which Israel occupied in June 1967 as illegal under international law (including Article 49 of the Fourth Geneva Convention).

But the EU has done nothing to help the Palestinians whose territories are occupied illegally. On the contrary, the EU (and therefore England) continues to support Israel in a number of ways. According to the United Nations half the Palestinian population in the occupied territories are unemployed and two thirds are living below the poverty line. A quarter of Palestinian children are suffering from acute or chronic malnutrition. The Palestinian economy has been brought close to collapse.

England and the EU have continued to support Israel in many ways. Israeli military officers have been trained in England. English companies have supplied small arms, grenade-making kits and spare parts for armoured fighting vehicles, tanks and combat aircraft to Israel. England has supplied Israel with leg irons, electric-shock belts and chemical and biological agents.

Instead of attempting to persuade its leaders to respect the law, the EU has continued to give Israel preferential trade treatment worth billions of pounds a year. In 2003, EU ministers agreed to further open EU markets to Israeli exports. The EU has banned the political wing of the Palestinian organisation Hamas and has put its leaders on a terrorist blacklist. The EU has curbed charities raising funds for Palestinians.

There is a strong argument that England supports Israel, and ignores the injustices done to Palestinians, in order to please the Americans. But in this instance our political stance is directly in line with EU policy.

## 235

Why are the Israelis allowed to perform in the Eurovision Song Contest?

Just asking.

## 236

Tim Coates, the former boss of Waterstone's bookshops, who was commissioned to produce a report on libraries by the libraries charity Libri, says that councils spend £24 every time they buy a £10 book because of the bureaucracy involved. He forecasts that libraries will be closed in 15 years.

I believe we can blame this tragedy and dilution of the quality of life in England squarely on the European Union. It is largely thanks to EU employment policies that libraries now spend 54% of their budgets on staff and just nine per cent on books.

## 237

*'Europe's nations should be guided towards the superstate without their people understanding what is happening. This can be accomplished by successive steps, each disguised as having an economic purpose, but which will eventually and irreversibly lead to federation.'*
JEAN MONNET (A FRENCH FOUNDER OF THE EU)

## 238

Labour and the EU want to ban political parties which they consider to be inappropriate or unsuitable.

## 239

*'Socialism is usually defined as 'common ownership of the means of production'. Crudely: the State, representing the whole nation, owns everything, and everyone is a State employee.'*
GEORGE ORWELL (THE LION AND THE UNICORN)

## 240

Thanks to EU directives on the disposal of rubbish, householders in England are now paying more and more for a constantly deteriorating service. Many people living in England now have their rubbish collected just once a fortnight. When a householder telephoned his local council to point out that rubbish left uncollected for two weeks was smelling badly and attracting rats he was told that he should double wrap every item of rubbish in plastic and then place the doubled wrapped items in a double layer of black plastic sacks. It did not seem to occur to the council official that this would dramatically increase the amount of waste.

Despite the EU regulations, millions of householders in France and Spain still have their rubbish collected daily.

## 241

Anyone who has ever lived in France or Germany will confirm that the French and the Germans have always been keen on paperwork and on officials. Ever since forms and uniforms were invented the French and the Germans have led the world in both. It is, therefore, hardly surprising that the EU (a creation of the new Franco-German alliance) should thrive on paperwork and officialdom.

We, in England, have never been quite so keen on bits of paper or on people in uniform. We like queuing (something that neither the Germans nor the French know how to do properly) but we regard administration as an unavoidable evil rather than a purpose in life.

But there is a twist.

The French and the Germans don't take the administrators seriously. They fill in forms by the dozen but no one takes any notice of them. Their streets are packed with officials in uniform but no one takes much notice of them either.

We, on the other hand, tend to take officials and paperwork

very seriously. We treat both with a good deal more respect than do the French or the Germans.

An English functionnaire will insist that the rules be followed to the letter. A French functionnaire will show you the loopholes. English citizens are brought up to play by the rules. French and German citizens are taught that the rules are merely a starting point for negotiations.

It is these fundamental variations in our history, and our outlook, which help explain why England is simply not suited for membership of the EU.

# 242

Our masters at the EU have made it clear that they now regard 'tax avoidance' as just as evil a sin as 'tax evasion'. This will surely mean that the Government's own 'National Savings' scheme will have to change its promotional literature.

A leaflet advertising the 'Cash Mini ISA', promoted by National Savings, says: 'You work hard for your money. And the income you receive has already been taxed once. So why let yourself be taxed on the interest earned by any savings you manage to put away? Opening a cash mini ISA with National Savings and Investments is just like opening a normal savings account, only you don't pay tax on the interest you earn. Now that sounds like a good idea.'

Sounds like a pretty straightforward incitement to avoid paying tax to me.

How long before the EU takes the Labour Government to court for encouraging tax avoidance?

# 243

Have you noticed that an increasing number of shops now make their customers queue for service? Shops which always used to have enough till operators to cope with all but the severest rush now have ropes and barriers built so that a queue of customers can snake around the shop.

Blame the EU for this unpleasant development. Employment legislation means that employers now have to get by with minimum staffing levels. It is cheaper to make customers wait, rather than to provide enough staff.

Another example of life getting worse for ordinary citizens because of the EU.

## 244

It is entirely because of regulations thought up by unelected bureaucrats in Brussels that so many shops, doctors' surgeries and other places now close at lunchtime (the very time when working people need to use them).

## 245

*'Once a country applies to join the EU, it becomes our slave.'*
EU OFFICIAL IN BRUSSELS

## 246

Will the EU allow England to continue to have sports teams? I very much doubt it. There will be no place for England in the new United States of Europe. How long have the English cricket, soccer and rugby teams got if we stay in the EU? No more than a decade at most.

## 247

The people supporting the EU claim to be progressive, liberal intellectuals. In practice, of course, they are not progressive, liberal or intellectual.

## 248

It is hardly surprising that conspiracy theories are rife in Europe. There are almost as many conspiracy theories about the real reasons for the existence of the EU as there are theorists.

The problem is that once the public lose trust in the people to whom they have given 'power of attorney' over their freedom, anything goes; no conspiracy theory is too outlandish to be believed.

## 249

The EU is a confused and confusing mess of an organisation.

Tobacco companies have now been banned from sponsoring sporting events within the EU. A good thing too, you might agree.

But for decades the EU has been paying out the best part of £1 billion a year in subsidies to European tobacco farmers. The subsidies are paid – and, I would point out, are still being paid – so that farmers within the EU can grow cheaper tobacco.

Even more bizarrely, the subsidies are paid for producing tobacco for which there is no market within the EU.

Much of the tobacco the EU farmers grow is of poor quality; being so rich in tar and nicotine that it is unsuitable for sale within the EU.

So what happens to the particularly dangerous type of tobacco which the EU encourages farmers to grow?

You're not going to like this.

This particularly dangerous, and subsidised tobacco, is dumped on poor Third World and Eastern block countries. It's relatively cheap for them to buy because (wait for it) it is subsidised by European taxpayers (that's you and me) through the EU.

Makes you proud to be a European, doesn't it?

## 250

There are only two types of EU supporter: the crooks and the fools.

## 251

We buy more from the other EU countries than we sell to them. (The total deficit is now around £175 billion.) This means that we pay the EU billions of pounds a year for the privilege of spending our money on their goods. Make no mistake about it, they need us far more than we need them. When we leave the EU the remaining members will still be desperate to trade with us.

## 252

The EU wants to force all service providers to store customers' Internet and phone data for up to three years. The information stored will include not just what was said, but where you were when you said it, lists of all the web sites you visited, details of all your text messages and e-mails and details of everyone with whom you communicated.

The very fact that bureaucrats should even ask for this type of information to be kept is an outrage. But our politicians are, as usual, rolling over.

England's Home Office (which supports this ultimate Big Brother intrusion) claims that: 'We are aware that organised crime and terrorist activity takes place across international boundaries and for that reason the Government is keen to see the harmonisation of data protection laws that prevent criminals finding a safe harbour within the EU.'

Only the EU or the fascist American Government (which is, incidentally, now planning to give itself access to hundreds of millions of international bank accounts around the world) could dream of anything this intrusive.

Intelligence experts agree that what they need is good information based on specific threats rather than mass surveillance which will merely produce far more data than anyone can ever usefully analyse.

But neither the EU nor the Labour Government really believe that collecting this sort of information will stop terrorists.

They want to snoop on honest citizens so that they can make sure we are obeying all their laws, paying all their fines and paying all the taxes they want from us.

Moreover, they will make a profit by selling the information to commercial companies wanting to build up even more complete pictures of the consumers they are targeting.

The end result, of course, will be less not more security – both for nations as well as individuals.

It goes without saying that other Government departments and agencies (such as the Customs and Excise and the Inland Revenue) will enthusiastically help themselves to this information.

The proposed legislation is almost certain to go through because individual countries in the EU will argue that all they are doing is 'harmonising'.

Companies already store much of the information which the EU now wants. They store it for billing purposes and to comply with data protection laws (which don't seem to me to have much to do with protecting the public or protecting the data).

The costs of storing all this data will, of course, be the responsibility of individual companies (who will, presumably, be able to share in the profits from selling the information on to outside agencies.) Naturally, in the end the net costs will be met by customers and shareholders.

We will be paying for the EU to spy on us.

# 253

Many of the new taxes introduced by the Labour Party are, in fact, taxes invented by the EU. Our politicians are merely doing what they have been told to do and implementing EU law.

The EU has an unquenchable appetite for money (largely because it is now an irredeemably corrupt organisation) and it has, therefore, devised a great many new tax raising regulations. If we remain in the EU we will find ourselves paying many more new 'stealth' taxes.

One suggestion, for example, is that there should be an EU tax on computer ownership and use.

# 254

Despite the fact that wind power is unlikely ever to contribute a noticeable amount of energy to our needs, the EU has stated its enthusiasm for windmill generated electricity. Naturally, the Labour Party is therefore also keen on wind power and has publicly expressed its determination to expand the number of wind farms in England.

However, in December 2004 it was reported that Prime Minister Tony Blair had helped block plans to build a wind farm near his Sedgefield constituency home.

More than 3,100 homes would have been supplied with 'green' electricity if an energy company had been allowed to build four wind turbines a mile from Mr Blair's house.

But when the plans emerged Mr and Mrs Blair used their not inconsiderable influence to support the opposition. The Sedgefield wind farm was rejected despite that fact that there had been 'strong professional recommendations in support of the project'.

## 255

It was French writer Voltaire who, in the 18th century, pointed out that: 'In general, the art of Government consists in taking as much money as possible from one group of citizens to give it to another.'

Voltaire realised that if you take money from Peter and give it to Pierre then it's a pretty fair guess that Pierre will like you quite a lot. If you do this repeatedly then Pierre is likely to expect the generosity to continue. Peter, however, is likely to become rather resentful.

## 256

Thousands of copies of my book *England Our England* have been sent to MPs, MEPs and to europhiles. I have received numerous letters from readers who have told me that they have gone through each fact and claim in the book looking for errors. But that they have failed to find any.

## 257

There are many EU supporters around who claim that the EU is democratically run, and that the European Parliament ensures that the wishes of the people of Europe are respected.

That is, to put it politely, a lie.

It isn't a teeny weeny little white lie.

It's a massive, twenty mile wide, five mile high, stinking, dirty black lie.

And here's a simple, single, specific example which shows that it is the unelected bureaucrats – not the political representatives – who have the power in the EU.

The people of Europe have, in numerous opinion polls, shown that they do not want to eat genetically modified food. And, in response to this feeling the EU had planned to introduce strict regulations which would have protected

European citizens from this threat.

But just weeks before the stricter regulations were due to come into force the unelected European Commission overruled the European Council of Ministers and the European Parliament (the one which is full of elected MEPs), and authorised the import of genetically modified maize for the manufacture of human food – either as whole sweet corn or as tinned sweet corn.

Why did they do this?

Simple.

The USA was putting a lot of pressure on the Commission.

And so the Commission caved in.

(You might now understand why the Labour Government has shocked even its own supporters by ignoring public protests and insisting that we accept genetically modified food. The Government had no alternative. Once again, the EU bureaucrats have spoken.)

There have been no tests on the long-term effects of eating genetically modified food. There have been too few tests on the possibility of consumers developing allergy reactions. There has been no adequate toxicological testing.

But, even though we, the voters, have made it perfectly clear that we are opposed to it, we now eat genetically modified food.

And we have to hope that nothing terrible happens.

Because no one knows whether it will or not.

The only thing I can tell you for certain is that the bureaucrats who made this decision are, like all EU employees, immune from prosecution for life. They cannot be prosecuted, whatever they have done. Even if they can be shown to have broken the law they are still immune.

The EU bureaucrats are untouchable and above the law.

If you care about justice, liberty, truth, humanity and your health then the EU and the Government are your enemy.

## 258

Thanks to the EU, England could well be in the dark soon.

Around a quarter of England's electricity comes from nuclear power stations – all but one of which are due to shut in the next two decades. They are old and need replacing. It takes at least a decade to set up a replacement nuclear power station.

So, it is clear that if nothing is done very quickly the lights will start going out in England within a few years.

The only sensible solution is to 'go nuclear'. Leading environmentalists such as James Lovelock (the inventor of the Gaia hypothesis) reckon that we will never be able to obtain enough electricity from wind, wave and solar power and must start building more nuclear power stations.

But the Labour Government and the EU are worried about nuclear power. They think terrorists might hijack a power station and drive it to Brussels.

So we're doing nothing about our impending shortage of electricity.

But, thanks to the EU, there is another little problem which seems guaranteed to turn our coming emergency into a real crisis. The EU has told England that two thirds of our coal-fired supply plants must shut down by 2011.

Since England gets 36% of her electricity from coal-fired supply plants this crisis is now already active.

You will be relieved to hear that France does not face this problem since the French get 80% of their energy from nuclear power and so the EU ruling does not worry them.

## 259

England's drinking laws are being revised to fit in with drinking laws throughout Europe.

The changes are producing huge problems and there is much opposition to the introduction of 24 hour drinking, but the changes will continue so that there is continuity among EU regions.

The problems are developing because England's drinking hours have been restricted for years. Because of the restrictions many drinkers have got into the habit of binge drinking – trying to drink as much alcohol as they can before the pub or club closes. Newspapers and magazines have made heroes and heroines out of heavy drinkers.

In France, where cafes have been able to serve alcohol around the clock for many years, there is no culture of binge drinking.

Attempting to impose French regulations on English drinking are proving (literally) fatal.

Given the opportunity to drink alcohol for 24 hours a day English drinkers will simply binge all day and night.

This is yet another example of the EU failing to understand the importance of national differences, and the impracticality and danger of imposing standard regulations on non-standard cultures.

## 260

No one seems to care much about patients these days. A four hour wait in casualty is officially considered acceptable. (Though I bet Tony Blair wouldn't have to wait that long if Leo had cut his leg or Cherie had broken her arm.) And whatever the fiddled Government figures might show hospital waiting lists are getting longer and longer.

The service patients get from GPs has also fallen dramatically.

If you can still get a doctor to come and see you at home at night or at weekends then you are one of the lucky few. Make the most of it because finding a doctor out of hours (any doctor – not just a good one) will soon be as big a long shot as winning the lottery. It will even make finding an NHS dentist look easy.

When I last practised as a GP (in the early 1980s), night and weekend visits were a routine and essential part of general practice. I was a member of what now would be considered a fairly small practice and our duty roster for out of hours calls meant that although our patients wouldn't necessarily see the doctor with whom they were registered they would at least see a local doctor, a doctor they knew, a doctor who knew how the local hospitals worked and who, if necessary, had access to the patient's medical history. Working nights and weekends and bank holidays wasn't fun but it was, it seemed to me, an essential and integral part of the job.

Today, most family doctors work office hours – which means that they are unavailable for 75% of the time. If you need your doctor outside office hours you will have to speak to an agency doctor who will probably be sitting in a call-centre some distance from your home, who will be on-call for a vast number of patients, who will know nothing about you, who will have no access to your medical notes and who will probably be reluctant to visit you at home.

Not by any stretch of the imagination can this be described as an improvement.

So, who is to blame for this dramatic reduction in the quality of medical care in England?

You've got one guess.

And if you guessed the EU you get full marks.

It was, of course, the EU which decided that working hours now have to be limited and that the hours a doctor is on-call have to be counted in with his working hours. EU regulations now limit the number of hours doctors can work and the English Government has had to give GPs the opportunity to opt out of emergency work.

Things aren't helped by the fact that thousands of doctors are retiring early – fed up of NHS red tape which makes their working lives miserable. And the problem has been exacerbated still further by the fact that the regulatory and taxation framework put in place by the EU and the Labour Government has encouraged many married women doctors to choose to work part-time. And that problem, in turn, has been made worse by the EU and the Government imposing a discriminatory quota system on universities and forcing medical schools dramatically to increase the number of women being accepted for medical training (regardless of their suitability).

In hospitals, the main problem is that nurses will be making the decisions which used to be made by doctors. Nurses will have to deal with emergencies. Nurses will have to perform procedures formerly performed by doctors. And nurses will have to make decisions on drug therapy.

It is, of course, sensible that doctors working hours should be limited. When I worked as a young hospital doctor I often worked over 100 hours a week. I once managed the maximum of 168 hours work in a single week. By the end of the work I was operating like a zombie.

Patients will benefit if doctors are less tired.

But the EU should have given governments more time to train the additional doctors who will be needed.

Once again the EU has screwed up.

This time their incompetence won't just cost us money. Thousands of patients will die unnecessary because of this cock-up: as nurses struggle to do work for which they have not been properly trained.

The only thing I can promise you is that if a Labour Minister (or his or her family) need medical care teams of fully qualified doctors will be on hand day and night.

I can safely guarantee that if Cherie Blair falls ill her life won't depend upon the quality of a life-or-death decision being made by a harassed, partly trained nurse.

On the other hand, unless your name is Blair, Blunkett, Straw or Prescott your life might.

## 261

While English taxpayers die in their thousands because hospitals take too long to perform basic tests (such as simple X-rays and blood tests) and uncomplicated, life-saving surgery, the EU and the English Government conspire to waste yet more money on pointless meetings.

In June 2005, it was revealed that Labour had, at an estimated cost of around £500,000, booked more than 100 rooms at a five star hotel so that EU officials and health ministers from other EU countries (and their accompanying officials) could spend a weekend together.

But what were they meeting about?

In the summer of 2005, it was not believed that the EU had any influence whatsoever over health care in individual countries. So, either the EU officials were meeting to discuss ways to standardise health care throughout Europe. Or, they were just meeting (at the expense of English taxpayers) to have a jolly good time.

The meeting was organised to take place during the time when the English Prime Minister was President of the European Union.

## 262

There are many in Europe who seem to believe that a genuine United States of Europe can be created out of a group of disparate nations (with entirely different cultures, histories, interests and enthusiasms) and that the result will be a single country along the lines of the United States of America.

This is, of course, complete baloney and only a complete idiot could believe it.

There are several reasons why it won't work.

The USA has a common language, a national identity, a shared history, a national media and a population which feels comfortable about moving about from one part of the country to another. The separate countries of Europe have well-established identities and a lot of very different histories and cultures. The citizens of France, Germany, Italy and England don't want to be citizens of a European superstate. The vast majority still think of themselves as being French, German, Italian or English rather than 'European'. Find me someone who calls themselves a 'European' and I will show you an EU employee.

Political debate within Europe still remains primarily national (with individual countries looking out for their own interests) and although the EU has ensured that most of the barriers to free and easy movement have been lifted (on the mainland continent at least) most EU citizens still live in the country where they were born. Ninety nine out of every hundred 'Europeans' still live in the country of their birth. People remain loyal to the country of their birth and not to Europe.

There is widespread resentment at the changes brought about by the EU. The French are worried that they are losing control of an organisation (the EU) which was created by the French. The Austrians are concerned because huge endless convoys of lorries now trundle across fragile Alpine passes carrying butter and other commodities on an endless tour of Europe. The vast number of regulations introduced to make the single market work have aroused resentment and contempt. In England there has been anger at the prosecution of market traders for selling produce in pounds and ounces rather than in EU approved metric weights. Dutch window cleaners were horrified and angry when they discovered that their ladders were too long to comply with EU health and safety regulations. Dutch houses are often higher than in other countries. How are the window cleaners supposed to clean the windows? The French and the Germans are angry that not all the red tape imposed on businesses in their countries has yet been imposed on businesses in the UK – which are, therefore, seen as operating at an advantage. None of this hatred and contempt for the EU is helped by the widespread belief that EU institutions, employees and spending programmes are both wasteful and corrupt.

But it is the language problem which will, above all others, ensure that there will be no United States of Europe.

Most European citizens speak only their native tongue. And any attempt to create a European language will fail. The original plan was to avoid national pride by replacing individual languages with Esperanto. That, of course, was a dismal failure.

As the number of EU nations grows so the language problems grow. The EU has become a bonanza for interpreters. The rules of the EU mean that every new law and every new piece of piffle has to be translated into every language and so there is an almost unquenchable thirst for translators who can translate Greek into Danish and Norwegian into Romanian. The EU should have been named Babel.

Does anyone honestly believe that the French will give up their language and accept English as the 'main' European language? Does anyone believe that the Germans or Italians will allow their languages to take second place to Spanish or English? Does anyone really believe that the good citizens of Leeds can be persuaded that in future they must conduct all their business in Greek?

## 263

Europhiles claim that the EU has helped create peace and prosperity and freedom. This, of course, is a neat piece of mythology created to provide a *raison d'être* for an organisation which has cost its members billions of pounds in membership fees and provided nothing but an endless stream of red tape and unwanted legislation in return. There is no evidence that the EU has created peace in Europe and it is patent nonsense to claim that without the bureaucrats in Brussels the French and the Germans would, by now, have been fighting World War III. Any prosperity which has been enjoyed has been a result of the same global factors which have led to rising productivity and increased trade in Asia and the USA. The English Government boasts endlessly about the economic miracle which has enabled them to reduce unemployment figures but in reality, of course, their so-called economic miracle is nothing more than an absurd Ponzi scheme, built on sand and destined to collapse. The reduced unemployment figures are a result not of prosperity but of the development of a variety of dishonest schemes designed to massage the figures down by putting the unemployed on 'schemes', allowing millions of cheats and fraudsters to take themselves off the unemployment register and describe themselves as long-term sick, and the fact that the only big employer who has been hiring recently has been the Government itself. (Since Labour acquired power in 1997 around a million manufacturing jobs have been lost. In that same period around a million new civil servants have been hired. As I have pointed out earlier, the Labour Ministers might not be clever, honest or genuinely creative but they are crafty enough to realise that people who receive their monthly pay cheque from the Government or whose survival depends upon Government benefits of one sort of another are quite likely to vote for the Government every time there is an election. Civil servants don't want to vote for a Government which might cut back Government spending, and the millions receiving benefits don't want to vote for a Government which might cut back the benefits budget.)

Freedom has come from individual revolutions (in Central Europe, Greece and Spain) which were nothing whatsoever to do with the EU.

Far from helping to create peace and prosperity and

freedom the only available evidence suggests that the EU is likely to damage all these.

England's independence and democracy is clearly threatened by the thousands of new laws coming from institutions in Brussels over which English electors have absolutely no control. Divisions between member states over the rights and wrongs of supporting American imperialism and starting wars all over the place have created tensions between member nations of the EU which probably would not have existed if the members were stand-alone countries.

The dispute over the illegal invasion of Iraq revealed that the EU is split into two quite separate factions. The one most closely identified with the French wants the EU to become an independent player on the world stage and to become a counterbalance to the power of the USA. The other, obviously identified with the English, wants to see the old western alliance, 'forged' during the Cold War, respected, maintained and strengthened.

The europhiles in the French Government fear the United States of America and believe that a united Europe may help hold back the more dangerous Americans. Blair and his colleagues believe that trying to create a counterweight to balance the power of the USA is both misguided and dangerous.

The split in the EU which resulted from the differing attitudes of the two factions was as much about a struggle for the control of the EU as it was a struggle for the oil in Iraq. The Spanish Government's decision to align itself with the USA and England (despite some 96% of Spanish electors opposing such a viewpoint) took place because the Spanish Government feared that it had for too long been dominated by the all-powerful Franco-German axis in European politics.

That part of the EU which opposes the power of the USA likes to point out that the EU spends far more on foreign aid than does the United States of America (which is one of the meanest countries in the world when it comes to giving away money without strings) but if this money has been given away to gain power it has been largely wasted.

The Americans have no respect for the EU. They despise the English, whom they see as weak, ineffectual and irrelevant, and they sneer at the French. They believe that Europe is in terminal decline with poor economic growth, declining fertility rates and a rapidly growing Muslim population. Immigration from Muslim countries, encouraged by the EU, has changed western Europe. Muslims now make up 7.5% of the French population. In Holland's four biggest cities most children under the age of 14 are Muslim, the children of immigrants from non-western countries. Europe's share of the world economy is visibly shrinking as the Asian economies accelerate. (The Americans do not yet see that their economy is also in decline and that the great days of American imperialism are as much a thing of the recent past as the great days of British imperialism are a thing of the distant past.)

The unnecessary regulations which are now accepted as an inevitable consequence of membership of the EU are destroying the European economy. Economically, the EU is falling behind the United States of America and looks backward moving when compared with dynamic, developing countries such as India and China.

It is the dangerous ambition of the most potent europhiles which is itself likely to create conflict, not so much between countries but within them. There has been a dramatic and potentially dangerous rise in the popularity of far right parties in most European countries in recent years and no one denies that this is a direct result of the oppressive yearning of a few bureaucrats for the formation of a European superstate. Just about every opinion poll in every EU member nation has shown that populations everywhere do not want or like the idea of a European superstate. In France, Germany, England and other countries there are great fears about the threat to jobs as immigrants from poorer parts of Europe take advantage of disappearing barriers. The citizens of those poorer countries, new members of the EU, are likely to take a dim view of their countries, which have only just won their independence, losing it again to the EU. There is, as I pointed out in my book *Saving England*, no difference between the old USSR and the new EU.

Finally, there are many experts who believe that the creation of the euro could create the political tensions which might eventually result in war.

## 264

*'We have before us an ordeal of the most grievous kind. You ask what is our policy? I will say: It is to wage war, by sea, land and air, with all our might and with all the strength that God can give us; to wage war against a monstrous tyranny, never surpassed in the dark, lamentable catalogue of human crime. That is our policy. You ask, What is our aim? I answer in one word: Victory. Victory at all costs, victory in spite of all terror, victory, however long and hard the road may be; for without victory, there is no survival. Let that be realised; no survival for the British Empire; no survival for all that the British Empire has stood for, no survival for the urge and impulses of the ages, that mankind will move forward towards its goal.'*
WINSTON CHURCHILL, 1940

## 265

If your car is fitted with a number plate disfigured with a small EU flag you can easily cover up the disfigurement with a Union Jack or a small replica of the cross of St. George.

## 266

Eurofanatics often claim that England would fall apart if we left the EU. This is nonsense. England could survive outside the EU very easily – and very successfully. Or we could establish a semi-detached relationship with the EU.

Other countries have done this.

Switzerland, for example, seems to have succeeded in negotiating an arrangement which gives the Swiss much of the upside of EU membership with none of the downside. The Swiss choose which projects to support financially (naturally, picking projects which will benefit Swiss interests) and retain their sovereignty. They can end their arrangement with the EU at any time.

Norway is now not a member of the EU and has chosen to cherry pick EU policies, opting out of the policies the country doesn't like and yet remaining as a member of the European Economic Area so that it can retain access to the EU's single market. In return for this purely commercial advantage, Norway has to accept the rules relating to the single market (without having a vote to decide what they are) and must pay a small annual fee to the EU budget. It is, presumably, fairly easy for the Norwegians to decide whether or not their annual fee is value for money. If the EU tries to push their fee too high the Norwegians can simply abandon their membership of the European Economic Area.

Those who seem to believe that the EU offers the only way forward should, perhaps, be aware that there is a powerful movement among French politicians who have had enough of the EU, who believe that the present, over-extended would-be United States of Europe is unwieldy and of no advantage to France, who believe that 'la difference' deserves to 'vive' and who would like to dissolve the present EU and start again with a much smaller group of countries. There are, indeed, many who believe that a Franco-German union would be best.

Similar feelings are commonplace in Germany where there

have long been plans for the day (now recognised as an increasingly likely possibility) when the EU implodes.

Naturally, neither France nor Germany will worry about England.

## 267

If, by now, you're not very angry then you haven't been paying attention.

## 268

We now need a referendum not on the EU constitution but on whether or not we should leave the EU. We need to leave the EU not just to regain our history and our culture but also to regain our freedom, our liberty and our independence. We need to leave the EU if we are to have any sort of future.

We need to leave the EU quickly – so that we get out before the EU collapses (which it will do). The EU is badly wounded but still dangerous. Now is the time to put it out of our misery.

When we leave the EU we will no longer have to obey the countless thousands of rules and regulations which govern countries which are members. But we must also make sure that we get rid of all the laws our governments have passed as a result of our membership of the EU.

Turning back the clock will change our nation.

We may even be able to recognise it again.

## 269

If you feel shocked or horrified by what you have read and you would now like to spread the word about the EU, and help save England, please tell your friends about this book. You can purchase additional copies to give away direct from Publishing House at special, low prices. For reasons which I have already explained, promoting and advertising a book which tells the truth is difficult these days. Promoting and advertising a book which tells the truth about the EU is particularly perilous and commercially hazardous. We do need all the help you can give us. Contact Publishing House (during normal office hours) for details of the special prices we offer to those who want to help spread the word.

For details of Vernon Coleman's books
please contact:

Publishing House
Trinity Place
Barnstaple
Devon EX32 9HG
England

Telephone     01271 328892
Fax           01271 328768

*Outside the UK:*
Telephone     +44 1271 328892
Fax           +44 1271 328768

*Or visit our website:*

www.vernoncoleman.com

# The Author

Instinctively anti-authority and recklessly uncompromising, Vernon Coleman is the iconoclastic author of over 90 books which have sold over 2 million copies in the UK, been translated into 23 languages and now sell in over 50 countries. His best-selling non-fiction book *Bodypower* was voted one of the 100 most popular books of the 1980s/90s and was turned into two television series in the UK. The film of his novel *Mrs Caldicot's Cabbage War* was released early in 2003. In the 1980s, although several of his books had been high in the best-seller lists, he got fed up with nervous publishers trying to edit all the good bits out of his books and so he started his own publishing conglomerate which began life in a barn and now employs five people.

Vernon Coleman has written columns for *The Daily Star, Sun, Sunday Express, Planet on Sunday* and the *People* (resigning from the latter when the editor refused to publish a column questioning the morality and legality of invading Iraq) and has contributed over 5,000 articles, columns and reviews to 100 leading British publications including the *Daily Telegraph, Sunday Telegraph, Guardian, Observer, Sunday Times, Daily Mail, Mail on Sunday, Daily Express, Woman, Woman's Own, Punch* and the *Spectator*. His columns and articles have also appeared in hundreds of leading magazines and newspapers throughout the rest of the world. He edited the *British Clinical Journal* for one year until a drug company told the publisher to choose between firing him or getting no more advertising. For twenty years he wrote a column which was syndicated to over 40 leading regional newspapers. Eventually, the column had to be abandoned when Government hired doctors offered to write alternative columns without charge to stop him telling readers the truth. In the UK he was the TV-am doctor on breakfast TV and wasn't fired until several weeks after a large food lobbyist had threatened to pull its advertising. He was the first networked television Agony Aunt. In the past he has presented TV and radio programmes for both BBC and commercial channels, though these days no producer who wants to keep his job for long is likely to invite him anywhere near a studio (especially a BBC studio). Many millions have consulted his Telephone Doctor advice lines and his web sites and for six years he wrote a monthly newsletter which had subscribers in 17 countries. Vernon Coleman has a medical degree, and an honorary science doctorate. He has worked for the Open University in the UK and was an honorary Professor of Holistic Medical Sciences at the Open International University based in Sri Lanka.

Vernon Coleman has received lots of unusual awards from people he likes and respects and regards as good eggs. He is, for example, a Knight Commander of The Ecumenical Royal Medical Humanitarian Order of Saint John of Jerusalem of the Knights of Malta and a member of the Ancient Royal Order of Physicians dedicated to His Majesty King Buddhadasa. In 2000, he was awarded the Yellow Emperor's Certificate of Excellence as Physician of the Millennium by the Medical Alternativa Institute. He is also Vice Chancellor of the Open International University.

He worked as a GP for ten years (resigning from the NHS after being fined for refusing to divulge confidential information about his patients to State bureaucrats) and has organised numerous campaigns both for people and for animals.

Vernon Coleman is balding rapidly and is widely disliked by members of the Establishment. He doesn't give a toss about either of these facts. Many attempts have been made to ban his books but he insists he will keep writing them even if he has to write them out in longhand and sell them on street corners (though he hopes it doesn't come to this because he still has a doctor's handwriting). He is married to Donna Antoinette, the totally adorable Welsh Princess, and is very pleased about this.